NO EXCUSES

HOW ANYONE CAN OVERCOME A ROUGH START

Copyright © 2020 Roger Auger

All rights reserved. No part of this publication may be reproduced, distributed, or transmitted in any form or by any means, including photocopying, recording, or other electronic or mechanical methods, without the prior written permission of the publisher, except in the case of brief quotations embodied in critical reviews and certain other noncommercial uses permitted by copyright law. For permission requests, write to the publisher, addressed "Attention: Permissions Coordinator," at the address below.

Roger Auger
27 Blackburn Lane
Hamilton Ontario
rocketrogerproperties.ca

ISBN: 978-1-7770889-0-3 (print)

Ordering Information:

Special discounts are available on quantity purchases by corporations, associations, and others. For details, contact Roger Auger.

TABLE OF CONTENTS

CHAPTER 1
We Need You.. 1

CHAPTER 2
I Had a Dream 5

CHAPTER 3
The Bottom of the Heap 15

CHAPTER 4
Helping Children Help Society —
It Starts with You... 27

CHAPTER 5
Mac and Cheese Scams..................................... 37

CHAPTER 6
The First Step into a New Life.......................... 51

CHAPTER 7
Handling the Haters 79

CHAPTER 8
Building Equity and Cashflow
with Real Estate 91

CHAPTER 9
Help Others—Feed Your Soul..........................105

CHAPTER 10
Boats and Rolexes—Getting Your Goals.......... 115

CHAPTER 11
It's Time to Act—We Need You
More Than Ever 119

Dedicated to the ones that go out of their way to help others. The ones who put in the effort and believe the world can be better.

NO EXCUSES

HOW ANYONE CAN OVERCOME A ROUGH START

ROGER AUGER

CHAPTER 1
WE NEED YOU

If you're a young person reading this and someone told you you'll never amount to anything, don't listen to them. **You are important to the world, and we need you.**

Use insults or lack of support from anyone as motivation.

If someone tells you you're worthless, the secret is it's because they feel worthless. In fact, right now, out loud, tell them to F%$# off. Also, tell them for me too. Because they're wrong. You can be a success no matter your background.

Almost everyone in my life told me I wouldn't amount to shit. My parents' insults were the loudest.

Their predictions for my future? Deadbeat, loser, failure, criminal, and lowlife. That was on a good day.

Turns out, they couldn't have been more wrong. I'm none of those things. Even with a limited education and parents who wanted me to fight more than they wanted me to go to school, I'm a successful real estate businessman today with an incredible, loving, and caring family and a happy life.

At this point in my life, I don't care what anybody says about me but at one time I did. I know how it feels to be a kid growing up with no support. That's why I wrote this book—to give hope to young people like you who don't realize how important and talented you are. *Everyone* has potential. You will have some ups and downs but your future will be amazing. It has to be because we need you.

Thank You For Helping Out

For those who are reading this with someone in mind who could use a little help, let me thank you now. Tough childhoods come in all shapes and sizes. And there are so many kids growing up without emotional or financial support. Many are even getting abused in the worst ways and they don't know that it is not normal. They don't know to ask for help because they think everyone goes through these things.

Child abuse and neglect is more common than you might think. And it's not just sexual or physical abuse. Many kids are deeply damaged by emotional abuse.

It's hard to find a statistic on the number of kids who undergo emotional abuse. Figures vary widely from source to source, but just to give you a sense, the *National Post* reported that 1 in 3 children experience some kind of abuse.[1] "Abuse" is such a broad term: It can mean sexual, physical, or emotional. Neglect falls in there too.

- The Red Cross has some additional stats:

- 31 percent of males and 21 percent of females experienced physical abuse during childhood.[2]

- Neglect is the most common form of abuse children suffer.[3]

The National Post article quoted Tracie Afifi, lead study author and professor of Community Health Sciences and Psychiatry at the University of Manitoba. "All types of child abuse were associated with all mental disorders, including suicidal thoughts and suicide attempts," she said.

You may not have realized that a third of the population waits until later to report that they experienced some kind of abuse as kids. They don't report it when it's happening because they don't realize they are being abused. Like I told you, I thought my life was normal and that everyone else was experiencing some version of my terrible upbringing. Kids don't know.

It's a bigger problem than many realize. And that's why we need you.

It's not easy sharing what I've experienced or sharing

[1] https://nationalpost.com/news/canada/one-third-of-canadians-have-suffered-child-abuse-highest-rates-in-the-western-provinces-study-says.

[2] https://www.redcross.ca/how-we-help/violence-bullying-and-abuse-prevention/educators/child-abuse-and-neglect-prevention/facts-on-child-abuse-and-neglect.

[3] https://www.redcross.ca/how-we-help/violence-bullying-and-abuse-prevention/educators/child-abuse-and-neglect-prevention/facts-on-child-abuse-and-neglect.

the things my family has done. I'm doing it with one simple goal: I want to help at least one child.

People who haven't experienced or witnessed abuse sometimes cannot fathom what happens to some children or the situations abused children deal with. It is beyond their ability to comprehend. Of course, you've heard stories of horrific parents. In many cases, kids are taken away for their own protection.

But in other instances, there are other families where the situation is on the precipice of legal and illegal or between dangerous for kids and just uncomfortable for them. Those are home situations bad enough to draw attention but not bad enough to move the child to safety. **Families with a few good days but a lot of bad days. These kids need a voice too.**

Please use my story to understand the mindset of the young person in that situation. It's likely different than you can imagine. Once you know what it's like to be in the situation of an abused child and how little help and support most youths ever receive, you realize the power you have to offer them help. You have the ability to unlock their potential and give them the support that nobody else is giving them. And when you hear my stories, I hope you see that making a big difference will be easier than you think.

CHAPTER 2
I HAD A DREAM

The seeds of my success were planted when I was just a kid. I looked around and all I saw was poverty and fighting, day in and day out. I knew I had to get out.

When I was about 10 years old, I had the spark of an idea that would save me. I found out that people rented parts of other people's homes to live in. Once I learned about that, I started to see the opportunity to rent out houses everywhere.

For example, I noticed my uncle's house was two houses in one. He lived in the upstairs, but he had another complete home in the basement—kitchen, living room, everything. Two separate units! My uncle didn't rent out the basement, but I could see the potential. There was money to be made here, I was sure. (I eventually found out it was even better than I thought at first; one Christmas Eve, I learned he had *two* separate units in the basement. I knew that could make a lot of money.)

As soon as I realized people paid to rent space, I knew that was what I wanted to do—rent out our house so we could pay the mortgage. I was always looking for ways to pay for our house, even as an elementary school kid.

I didn't yet understand that paying for the mortgage (or the rent) was supposed to be the parents' job. My parents always "borrowed" money from me, so I didn't know they were the ones that were supposed to take care of me.

But I knew we couldn't rent out our wet, leaky basement. Our house was big, and old, with five bedrooms and an attic space. My family sometimes rented out rooms to people, but imagine what we could do with the whole house! That would bring in a lot of money. I evaluated the situation like an entrepreneur from the start and focused on the income potential. Never mind that renting our house would have left us homeless. At 10, I wasn't thinking that far ahead. The opportunity to make money was what stuck in my head.

Of course, we never did it. But this seed was now planted in my mind and I knew I would someday rent out houses to other people for money.

I was obsessed with rentals. When I went to friends' houses I would open the doors to their extra rooms and tell them that they should rent them for extra money. They always laughed. "Good luck with that idea," they said. Or just, "Shut up, Roger."

My idea was ahead of its time—I could've had the first Airbnb!

It wasn't so easy to realize my real estate plans. At least not right away. Not as a preteen boy.

So at 12, I turned my attention to making money. I worked lots of jobs and made money by selling stuff at a flea market on Sundays. The stores weren't open so it was the perfect day for me to sell used video games and used tools I collected during the week. I put an ad in the paper to buy used stuff from people to resell at the flea market. People would bring their things by the house and if it was a good price, I'd buy it. If not, I wouldn't. I ran my little stand at the flea market for three years. I did well, making between $300-$500 per week. When I was 15, the stores started to stay open on Sundays and the traffic got so slow at the flea market that it shut its doors. I lost my stand.

But I never stopped working, unless I was at school or football practice. I parked cars at football games and scalped tickets. It was better than going to work at McDonald's where they would never give me enough hours so I would have had to take another job at KFC.

The money I made was decent, but it didn't last long. I had to pay for my lunches at school, my laundry, and a majority of the family expenses, including my dad's chain-smoking habit. Cigarettes are expensive. Plus, my dad would borrow money from me and never pay it back. And I didn't know anything about saving money. School doesn't teach that and my family really didn't teach that. So if I wanted to keep having money in my pockets, I had to keep finding ways to make more.

Each day, I knew how much I had to make that day to

survive the day. That was my formula. What did I want to or have to buy that day and how much would it cost? Okay, how can I make that money?

Every day I went through that thought process.

Even as a kid, I knew there had to be a better way. I knew that it wasn't possible to keep working all the time like I was doing. I knew you had to have a way to make money all the time, even when you were sleeping, otherwise you'd never be able to retire. I didn't know how to do it, though.

As I got older, I noticed Donald Trump. He got my attention, of course, because he was out there as someone who got rich building, buying, and selling real estate. He was always on TV and seemed to have it all. Trump Tower was incredible and had my attention. I wanted to be like him.

I knew I wasn't—I found out his parents gave him money to start—but I was impressed every time another Trump building or golf course went up. Like him, I wanted to have it all. I also found Richard Branson inspiring because he would figure out what people wanted and then he'd find a way to get it for them. These guys showed me there were other ways to live and build up money than just working a regular job.

I kept busy as a teenage boy making money in whatever way I could, but when I left home at 18, I was still thinking about real estate.

Then I experienced my own real estate situation first-hand. The numbers made me see gold. I started renting a house with five roommates. Six of us were paying rent, and I did the math on what the guy who owned the house was making every month.

It was a lot of money. Knowing that didn't make me very happy. He was doing what I wanted to do. I was renting someone else's property, which was the opposite of what I wanted.

Trouble was, I didn't have rich parents to back me up, like Donald Trump. I didn't have an education in business either.

Still, I was determined. I believed in myself. I always have. In fact, in my family now, we all have necklaces with charms that say, "Believe in Yourself." When my kids are on the sports field, if they're struggling, I'm there in the stands pounding my chest, pointing to that necklace, reminding them that if they believe in themselves, they will excel.

It's not always easy to keep believing because other people will try to bring you down. My brothers and sisters, my aunts and uncles, they all said I was crazy to look for rental units. "You'll lose your shirt," they'd say. "You'll never make it."

I didn't listen to any of them. I listened to the one person who said something positive, my Uncle Bill. He owned his own business and told me to go ahead and try it. I saw he had a big house and employees, so it seemed like he knew what he was talking about, even though my parents had nothing good to say about him.

Banking on the Future

I've always stayed positive. But banks don't lend based on how many positive thoughts you have. They want to see cash in the bank and income.

In 2009 and 2010, when I wanted to start renting out houses, there weren't any banks that would deal with me. I didn't have enough saved.

Banks don't think outside the box, but I did. And the one thing I learned as a kid hustling to make money every day is that I just had to keep trying. I always find a way. So I didn't give up when the banks said no. I just kept finding ways to add income and make more money.

I also developed a relationship with a bank manager at my credit union. She knew how hard I worked—I had a full-time job and I owned several hot dog stands in those days—and she knew that I was trying to get a loan for a house.

It didn't happen instantly but after a while, when everyone else was turning me down for a loan to buy a house, she somehow made it happen. I don't know if my work ethic impressed her or if she had some secret knowledge about the loan officer that she threatened to release but I got that loan.

Some may have kicked back and relaxed with that win, feeling like they had now made it. But that wasn't me. Nope. I knew I needed to work even harder. I made double payments on the home for the next seven years. I could've wasted money on expensive furniture or food. Okay, I bought some food. But I saved as much as I could and invested it in new rentals whenever I could. I had the rental bug.

THIS IS IT! Becoming a Landlord at Long Last

Finally, I had enough equity in my first house to buy my first rental property. After all of the hustling. The long hours. The mustard and ketchup on my shirt, pants, hair, and underwear. (Yes, underwear. It happens to all hot dog vendors.) All of it had led to this moment. My dream was finally real—I had a chance to have a rental property.

We built up enough equity in our home to refinance it and take out enough money to then put a down payment on a new property that could become our rental property.

Of course, it wasn't that easy. And I'll explain the mechanics in a bit more detail in a few chapters so you understand how we saved the money and what we did to make this happen, but I want you to know that we did get there. But it wasn't the first bank that said yes. And even when I had a lot of the pieces the bank wanted in place, getting my first rental property was incredibly hard. The bank that held the mortgage on my home got nervous. Even with a lot of equity and value in my home, they were nervous about loaning me money to get the rental property.

I didn't give up. I checked with other banks.

Nope.

Nope.

No, no, no, no, no, yes, no, no.

Hey, wait. Yes?

Finally, a bank decided to lend us the money to get the second house. I rented the house out right away. Then with the remaining money I had from the refinance, almost immediately I bought a third house and rented it out to students. Now I had three houses and three banks.

Both rental houses were making cash. I paid as much as I could into the mortgage. And I kept looking for properties.

Right now, I know what you're thinking. This is where Roger buys too many houses and something bad happens and he loses them. Nope.

I kept buying houses. It wasn't long before I bought two more. I did refinances of mortgages and kept buying. I wasn't worried about mortgage fees or cancellation fees or any other fees. I believed in myself.

This makes it sound easier than it was. It wasn't. It's still not easy. I hit roadblocks all the time. But I figure out how to go around them. There is always a way. And hard work will get you around just about any road block. I was always looking for new opportunities. I knew I could make it work if I worked hard. I just had to keep renters in the homes so the payments would be made and the extra cash would allow me to buy even more.

I was rejected many times, but I knew how to build relationships. People would get to know me, understand what a hard worker I was, and help me out a little.

More people doubted me than supported me. It's too bad that there often are more haters than people who want you to succeed, at least where I came from. And so many people had doubted me, but here I was, doing exactly what I said I would.

I wasn't a deadbeat, a loser, or a criminal. I was a landlord. And I loved it. Everything about it. It isn't just the money. I love buying properties. **If you love what you're doing, you never feel like you're working.**

And if you want to buy rental properties like I did, I'll share more on how I did it later. For now, there's a little more I want to share in case you're where I was and need to know you're not alone. Because we really do need you. And there's a child with a dream somewhere who needs you too.

CHAPTER 3

THE BOTTOM OF THE HEAP

Have you ever watched a movie where the lead character suddenly realizes a shocking truth? You know what often happens…they can't believe they didn't know this glaring truth that everyone else seems to know and they fall to their knees and scream to the sky…

"I've been working for the bad guy this whole time!"

"I was switched at birth with another baby!"

"I'm…I'm a robot!"

I had my own version of that scene when I was about 17. I discovered that other kids my age didn't have to pay the mortgage for their parents!

Unlike in the movies, I didn't drop to my knees and scream to the sky.

Instead, I slowly looked around and relived my whole life before coming to terms with my new reality. I felt lost.

Then angry. Confused. Sad. Betrayed. Then lost again. I went through that process for about two or three…decades.

Learning What Normal Looks Like

I didn't understand that my life was different from others for a long time. It happened when I started dating a wonderful girl who was not from my part of town. I was from a low-income area. She lived on the mountain. We thought those people were high-class so we never mixed. They had yards, we had dirt. They had a recreation center, we had a strip club.

We connected at the roller skating rink. It was the cool place for kids at my school to hang out. She was quite a skater and I was very good at figuring out how to get up from the prone position. She introduced me to several people who are still my friends to this day. Friends for life.

I knew they were different than me but I still thought my life was normal.

Just so you know what I thought was normal:

Before I met the girl at the skating rink, my friends and I all had parents who were drunks, loved drugs, gambled, and fought with the neighbors (and everyone else, for that matter). Everywhere in the neighborhood there were beatings. They happened to my friends. To their moms. To their dads. To me. My mom. To my siblings. Does that seem strange to you? It didn't to us. That was just day-to-day life. It was normal and we didn't question it.

Of course, I watched TV and saw the families on TV were different, but I thought that was make-believe. It's TV! This was real life.

A normal day in my house might have started with breakfast and going to school, or maybe not. My parents didn't care if I went to school. If I felt like staying home, I stayed home.

Whether I was at home or at school, I'd probably end up in a fight with someone. Kids at school or my sister at home. If I made it to school, I either walked five or six blocks or took the bus, went to work, and walked back home.

Back at home, nobody talked much. I might hear stories from my mom about how bad her family was or who was fighting with who. There were no pleasantries exchanged about the weather or what we were learning in school.

I did pay attention to what day of the week it was, though. If it was Thursday or Friday, I would avoid going home if I could. Thursday was payday and my dad would be drunk. Or stoned. Or both.

He didn't hide his drug use from us at all. His house, his rules. Don't like it? Get out. I tried to stay out as much as I could—not going home unless I really had nowhere else to go. As soon as I was 18, he wanted to charge me rent (on top of the mortgage payments I was already making) so I moved out.

When I was home, I was my father's servant. We all were. He needed a beer, he needed coffee, he needed cigarettes, and someone had to go get them. That was me. Even as a kid, I bought cigarettes at the corner store.

If I didn't do it, there'd be a fight. There would be a fight anyway, actually. That was my mom's life—fighting with anyone and everyone, all the time. My sister was violent, too, and my brother hung out with the wrong people and had such low self-esteem. We all fought with each other, and not just with words. With fists.

My parents were always pushing me to find ways to make money because I was the kid and I was supposed to be paying the bills. It made sense to me. I'm living in their house, why should I get a free ride? I didn't think that was strange. It had been this way since I was little. They didn't care how I made money or if I broke the law doing it.

People in my family didn't usually have jobs. If they did, they didn't keep them. Instead, they had a lot of scams going on. I don't think I even knew half of what was really going on but I remember one. Through some sort of gang connections, my dad got hold of a tractor-trailer load of Kraft macaroni and cheese. Those boxes filled an entire two-car garage. Now, I love a Kraft dinner as much as anyone else but we didn't eat *that* much macaroni and cheese.

It wasn't for us. It was for sale. The deal was, I would go door to door and sell Kraft dinners to the neighbors. I did great, actually. **We were *the* black market source for Kraft dinners.** Half the garage was empty in just a few days.

Then, and this is probably the reason I remember this

scam so well, there was the day that the police arrived at the front door. Not a friendly visit. They were raiding our house!

They found the stash: Thousands of boxes of Kraft dinners. My dad managed to blame it on someone renting the garage space, but the mess was all over the local paper. All the school kids knew about it the next day, and I got bullied worse than ever.

There are kids in the world right now who don't realize they are in abusive and dangerous situations. They are just playing the cards they're dealt—just like I was—and we need to find them and help them.

I didn't know any better, and nobody told me. Not my father, who drove a bus on his best days, but otherwise drank and did drugs and blamed everyone else for his dreams not coming true. That's a common theme among my entire family: their life not going their way is *always* someone else's fault.

My mother, who fell for the dreamer side of my father, went off the deep end when she discovered what kind of person my father really was. She was undiagnosed bipolar and didn't have an education.

So who could help me? Not my brother. My brother, the straight-A genius who got those grades without ever studying, always knew exactly when to leave the house—right before the beatings began. I was too young to escape. My sister was no help either. She just got out of the way as much as she could; mostly we boys were the punching bags.

With a bitter and mean drunk father, a crazy mother, and siblings trapped in the same hell in a part of town where it all seemed normal, I couldn't see how wrong it was. Other people would take one look and think they were watching some sort of dystopian movie where society has collapsed. It all seemed perfectly normal to me.

Fortunately, just up the hill was another reality.

Going Up the Mountain

When I reached the age where I started dating, I started to understand our family was different. I still didn't have a full picture, but there was part of me that knew where I came from wasn't right, and I was embarrassed. I kept my family life as hidden as was humanly possible.

It wasn't easy keeping my worlds separate. I began dating Allison, the girl from up on the mountain, where the families were well-educated and lived in much nicer homes. Some of my friends called me a traitor. How could I date this girl? A mountain girl?! What was wrong with me, associating with those snobs?

They weren't snobs. We thought they looked down on us in our poor neighborhood but honestly, we didn't even register in their minds. They lived in a whole different world.

I first saw it when I walked into Allison's house. It was a good-sized, middle-class home. I thought it was a mansion. Her father worked and had a good job. Her mother worked some, too, but also stayed home at times with the kids. In this family, they talked to each other. Talked!

Their conversations were polite and pleasant, and there was no yelling. I couldn't believe it. I didn't believe it, actually. I figured they were on their best behavior.

I waited for someone to punch somebody else.

I thought surely the fights would happen at dinner. The parents each had a glass of wine with dinner. Surely there would be a drunken brawl by the end of the meal. But no. They didn't get wasted and were in full control of themselves. That was the first time in my life I saw a family that actually behaved like a happy family. Like what I'd heard a normal family was. Kind of like the TV families.

I still wasn't convinced. I was pretty sure that violence would break out any minute.

Instead, her parents asked their kids about their days and suggested that they should get their homework done. My parents told us *not* to do homework and didn't even care if we went to school. Less schoolwork meant more paying work, and I was supposed to be making as much money as I could.

Sitting at this dinner, part of me never wanted to go home again. At my house, the only conversation was, "Move your head—you're blocking the TV." Or, "Get me the salt."

Listening to this family chatting with each other was freaking me out. I thought, "What's wrong with these people? Are they acting?" I was a little disoriented. Were they putting on a show?

I had only seen this behavior on TV! And we had always thought TV shows were lies.

Being with this family was breathtaking. How was I going to talk about this to anyone? Could I tell my friends about this? Nope. **My buddies from the neighborhood were already calling me a traitor, and they thought I was acting like I was better than them.**

My parents would kill me just for mentioning I had been there. They probably didn't want me to know that most kids actually got presents on their birthdays, not just promises like, "It's on layaway." I'm certain they didn't want me to stop paying the mortgage.

I couldn't make sense of it all. Allison's family seemed too good to be true. Then I figured it out. This mountain dad and mom wanted something from me.

But what?

Their daughter had told them I was a hustler. So they must be playing me for some money. Same with my new mountain friends. I had to find out what they wanted from me. I tucked my money safely away in my pocket. I wouldn't let them scam me into anything.

When we went back to their house, they stuck with the plan and were very nice to me, just like those liars on the TV shows. I didn't let down my guard, though. Then the next time I went over, they were nice and supportive again. And the next time. The next. Next. Next. Next. These people were good. So patient with their scheme...

Same with my new buddies, the ones Allison introduced me to.

I figured that even if these guys came from a hoity-toity area, their home lives must be just like mine. I kept waiting for the truth to be revealed. They had to want me around for some reason. Soon they would reveal it.

But nothing happened. Little by little, I started to trust them. They thought I was cool. These new buddies knew that I was a guy who was always making money and was a hustler. They thought I must have a ton saved for college and were impressed that I'd bought my own car. They didn't know I was making our house payment and my father was about to steal my car and sell it.

They knew I was a fighter. I even defended them against the guys from my old neighborhood and they appreciated that.

But we were both out of our comfort zones.

If there ever were situations where they would be in the same room or even the vicinity as my family, they avoided my parents. This didn't happen very often, but sometimes when I was running the hot dog carts for charity (I was 18), my friends would come and help me and my parents would come to get free food. My friends kept their distance from my parents. I don't know if they had heard the stories about my house or they didn't want a run-in with one of the crazies who haunted the neighborhood (like my mother). Some of my original friends had spilled the beans to everyone that my mom had chased them with a hammer one day and a two-by-four on another. My old friends thought that was hilarious. My new friends wouldn't.

This Is Real?

Even though I started to trust the friends from the mountain, I still thought they were sneaky and hiding something.

Then it hit me. What if they aren't faking it? What if this is how they really act?

They smiled. Hugged me. Gave advice. This can't be right.

Where were the judgments? Where was the yelling? They were just happy if I was happy. They didn't want anything. They weren't scamming me.

This was all real.

That pissed me off more than anything!

How'd I get the life I got? I want my life to be like this! I want to be a better person! I want to go to school! They're not more special than I am! This is bullshit! In fact, I'm better than them! They wouldn't last five minutes in my life! Fuck them!

I was never going to go back to that family to be with people who had it all. In my mind, they were just a rarity anyway. It was all handed to them. I started to blame everyone and everything for my situation.

The Missing Piece

My whole life I had been listening to my dad complaining and blaming others, never taking any responsibility for himself. Then one day, I was at a friend's house for a barbecue and all I was doing was complaining and being a jackass. I was bitching about owners and bouncers. Jeff looked at me weird and said, "You sound like your dad."

That pulled me up short so I decided to check around and see the real truth.

What is life supposed to be like?

I spent time talking to different kids in school and listening closely to the stories they told. Is this some kind of conspiracy? Is everybody in on it? WTF? Why is this happening to me?

I started sharing stories from my life with my new friends. I told them I worked several jobs at a time to pay the family's mortgage. They stared at me.

"You pay the mortgage?" one guy asked.

I said, "Yeah."

We had a sort of code. No matter what, you take care of your family and family comes first. So I was thinking, "Duh! I stay in my parents' house. I eat their food. I should have to pay."

The boy screamed, "You're their *kid*! They're supposed to take care of you!"

I was stunned. Really? That's how it was supposed to work?

It was if I lived in an upside down world.

And I did.

CHAPTER 4

HELPING CHILDREN HELP SOCIETY—IT STARTS WITH YOU

Depending on what your life is like right now, you might be thinking, "Wow, so Roger paid the family mortgage at age 12, could barely write because he was told not to go to school, had an alcoholic father who wanted him to sell drugs and a bipolar mother who beat his friend with a two-by-four, moved from school to school, worked 80 hours a week for 20 years doing menial jobs to barely eke out a living, and now he's made a lot of money in real estate and wants to be a symbol of hope to a young person."

Or you might be thinking I have some big upsell to hit you with where I am going to sell you on some expensive solution to your life challenges and tell you that if I can do it so can you. That's what I would have thought too. I never would have thought someone would spend thousands of dollars to get help writing a book just to help at least one child. I would have expected there to be a scam or a gimmick so I expect you to think that too.

But I hope you are like I was and just stay open to the idea that *maybe life can be different.*

My goal is simple. I want to help children who are living like I had to live. If you are one, or if you know one, I wrote this book for you.

Others may read this book to learn about real estate or just to hear my story, and I hope they do, but **I want to help the kids who are having a rough childhood.**

I want to help at least one child know that they can create the life they want to live, that what they are going through is not "just what life is like"—and that there are people who will help. I also want you to know that helping a child, or several, will do a lot for society.

Many of the people I grew up with are in the exact same place they were two decades ago. They are not contributing to society. They don't think anything can change so they don't try. They are always looking for handouts, and in most cases, draining the resources that are available to them and doing nothing to build them back up.

And they think that is just how life is.

It's not true. Your past doesn't have to dictate what's ahead for you. You can choose to make it better.

It's harder as an adult. Adults aren't as likely to ask for—and accept—help.

But kids, they need help. They need to know that life can be different or better.

As I've said, I didn't know I was different until much

later. I always thought everyone had an agenda. Kids growing up in situations like mine, or worse, don't know that all kids aren't raised like that. They don't know they can have dreams and put a plan in place to make them a reality. But the first thing kids have to know, or at least the thing I learned that saved me, was that I was the one who had to make the change. Nobody around me was going to change.

No Whining—Change Your Life

Shit happens. Some shit shouldn't happen, especially to kids, but it does. The point of this book is that you can come from a horrible situation and still do well.

You can change the direction of your life.

The pain often gets passed down from generation to generation. Your dad's dad beat him so he beats you. Then, all too often, the kid goes on to beat their kids too.

The same happens with alcoholism and verbal abuse.

That can stop here and now. You don't have to pass down the pain. In fact, you shouldn't.

You can do really well for yourself. And in doing well for yourself you will have the resources to help a child who's experiencing a rough childhood. I think you might feel you have a responsibility to help that child.

You can help others. You should help others.

It doesn't have to be big or complicated.

One simple thing I do to help others is give people

chances. I hire just about anybody to work on my houses. If they need someone to believe in them and give them a chance, I do. Sometimes that doesn't work out in my favor, but sometimes I help someone who really just needs a break. Often, it creates lifelong loyalty and that person becomes someone I can count on for anything, but that's not why I do it. I do it because if they are someone good who just needs a break, I want to give them the chance.

Maybe that person would be just fine without you. But, often, without a break or a bit of help they feel they have no choice but to take a more dangerous path. That can be even worse for children who don't know any better. Imagine how easy it would be for me to run hustles after learning that I can sell anything, even the stolen mac and cheese we had in our garage!

If the child from that kind of situation goes down the wrong path, it doesn't only hurt him or her: It hurts society as a whole. Crime. Scams. Incarceration. Drugs.

There's another key reason I want to tell you what went on in my family. Because, like most kids from insane households, it was the only thing I had ever been subjected to. I had no idea that what was happening in my life was not the norm. I know I said that already but it's so important: It's *why* you have to help children who are in these kinds of situations if you can. I didn't know which responsibilities were supposed to be the adults' and which were supposed to be the kids'.

I know I'm not the only one who has been through this kind of childhood. I want to let others know they're not alone.

But this book isn't about me. This book is about *you*. Maybe you feel like something is holding you back from following your dreams. That might be how it feels, but the biggest message I want to give you is that it's *you* holding you back. But you have the choice. You just have to first decide to change, then take action. Look at what I went through. And I did it.

It doesn't matter where you came from. You can do anything you want.

No Excuses

The excuses you have in your mind are roadblocks *you* are letting stop you. They're holding you back from being the person you can be or the best you can be. You can have whatever you like, or whatever you want in the future, and have fun doing it.

I'm not saying it is going to be easy. It's not! You cannot expect anyone to make it easy for you just because you had a hard start in life. Don't make excuses. Don't let the negative person down the street or in the next room bring you down. If you do, you are letting them win.

Move forward one day at a time. Do what you need to do. It won't happen overnight. That's okay.

Along the way, some people will do whatever they can to stop you. Granted, some will have good intentions and believe they are "protecting" you. But many will try to talk you out of succeeding—or even trying—because they are afraid to try. Don't let their negativity stop you. I struggle with writing because I couldn't go to school, and I've written this book. I had help. And that, too, is an incredible lesson—you don't have to do everything alone. In fact, some things you shouldn't try alone. I'll talk later in the book about the people I surround myself with and the amazing opportunities it's opened up for me in my life and my business.

Believe in yourself and work hard.

Write down what you want to accomplish and by which date. I've included an entire chapter on goal-setting because I think it's the single most important thing I've done to create the success I've had so far, including writing a book! I had to set a goal and a date and make sure I had what I needed to get started.

Break your goal down by years, then months, and then days.

If you do that, and never stop working hard, your goal—your dream—will come true, and day by day, it will become achievable. I guarantee it.

Nobody Owes You Anything

No matter what horrible thing has happened to you, there is nothing you are entitled to because of what happened to you.

Everybody has a story in life of what happened to them. Nobody is owed anything. You are not entitled to a free lunch just because of the past. Dwelling on the past doesn't help you succeed.

It pisses me off when I meet kids with opportunities to succeed whose sense of entitlement holds them back. You are holding yourself back.

I've been watching the news lately. The government cut the money away from disabled families and a lot of parents are pissed off because they think the government should pay for them and support their kids. The parents are saying, "Who is going to take care of my kid?" and "Who is going to help them?"

I wanted to yell at the TV, "*You* are going to take care of your kid!"

I'm not saying we shouldn't help people. And I am not saying that no government assistance should ever be given. That's not my point at all. I really just don't want you to expect to be helped. If the government stopped funding the program you're using, you would have to find a way!

You don't give up. It's not someone else's job to fix your problem. It's a benefit of our society that there are programs to help and support people who need it, but that doesn't mean that is the only way.

There is always a job. Maybe you think it's beneath you, but there is work. You have to do whatever it takes to support your family. And often, at least when you start out, that means doing work you don't want to do because it's what you have to do.

Looking at the government helplessly won't help you

find a solution. That kind of thinking stops people from finding a way to help themselves and help their kids. You aren't helpless.

What do you think you are entitled to? What are the reasons you're entitled?

Seriously, why do you think you are entitled to something you haven't worked for?

The only thing you're entitled to is what you do for yourself and what you create for yourself.

And just so you know, it's not just people relying on government subsidies who think this way.

Even people who are more comfortable financially suffer from this line of thinking. It's holding them back too. I was at an investment meeting recently. I overheard some investors talking about a deal I did where I turned a two-bedroom home that nobody wanted to buy into a six-bedroom, cash-making rental (I'll tell you about that one soon).

The would-be investor said to his friend, "Why doesn't anyone bring me deals like that? I should be getting deals like that!"

He's probably going to struggle because he thinks someone should give him a good deal. But nobody gave me anything in real estate. I worked for everything, and the good deals I've made were because I was out looking at a lot of properties and talking with a lot of people to find solutions to problems.

I'm not saying that you should never get temporary help. Some people need a boost. I think the best help is when someone teaches you something. It's that old saying you've heard before, "Give a man a fish and you feed him for a day. Teach him how to fish and you feed him for a lifetime."

So if someone really needs a hand, I think it's great to help someone. I do it all the time. But if they don't want to help themselves then it's not going to work. Permanent help doesn't work.

People find a way to take advantage of permanent help. I see it all the time where I come from. Instead of working, they work to find ways to never get a job and get paid for doing nothing. Tenants getting government handouts can work the system and either get paid cash under the table or keep their income low enough to keep the government subsidy. That's not a system that works. And if you're working that system right now, you're never going to get out and create a better life for you and your family.

You're just making excuses. There's always a way. I'm not saying it's easy, but there are always ways to get what you are dreaming about.

Ask for Lessons, Not Money

My nephew is really intelligent—he could read this book once and change his behavior. He didn't have a horrible upbringing but it wasn't easy. He didn't have a father figure. There wasn't anyone for him to really learn positive things from. He dropped out of school and started doing drugs. He wasted that great brain he's been given.

He should have called me and said, "Uncle Roger, you've been buying real estate and I know you got started with nothing. How'd you do it? Can you teach me?" Instead he basically said, "I had a hard life. You have done well, so can you give me a free place to stay so I can give my kid a home?"

He wanted a handout!

And you wonder why he thinks that way? I was at a family funeral recently. I was sitting there, minding my own business, when my brother started yelling at me from across the room, "Mr. Millionaire! Buy me a beer, now that you're so rich."

Why wouldn't my nephew think he should get a handout from me if that is what he's learning from the family around him?

If that is you, ask the person who is doing well to teach you, don't ask them for money. You can learn to do what they do; maybe even do it better. If they give you that free place to live or buy you a beer, you got something one time and you're always going to look for someone else to give you a handout.

CHAPTER 5
MAC AND CHEESE SCAMS

When you're young, you don't understand anything but what you're shown. You believe your parents: What they say must be true. Even if your parents are mean or violent, you still have love for them. They are your parents. And you see life through their lenses. If your parents are outcasts, you figure you must be an outcast too. You must be because that's how everyone else treats you too.

At some point, children do start to see that they aren't their parents. And just because a child is raised rough, that doesn't mean that is all they can be. If children really only learn what they live, I should never have learned to be a loving husband and father or a successful businessman. My story means there is hope for every child who is being beaten, starved, lied to, given false hope, and bullied over and over by peers, and even family.

Gifts on Hold

I didn't get presents for my birthday; I got promises. Every year, Mom would tell me she got me a present but that it was on layaway. She was paying for it over time and as soon as she was done, I'd get it. I usually didn't get it.

The year I turned six was different. I got a six-foot sub. Yes, a sandwich. So much food! It may not sound like much, but it was the best gift ever. I was so happy, and all my friends were so jealous. I was the only one around with a six-foot sub.

The next year, everything was "on layaway" again. I understand my mom couldn't afford gifts. If she'd just said so, it might've been better, but she just always made promises that never came true.

When I was eight, I was in love with chrome bikes. They were so shiny. I wanted one so badly. I showed one to my mom at the bike shop down the street so she knew just what I wanted.

When my birthday came, I was absolutely shocked because she actually got me what I wanted and it was there on my birthday!

I couldn't believe my eyes. There it was, my shiny silver bike. A chrome bike! I was so happy, I rode off down the street to show it off. Only the other kids laughed at me. It wasn't a real chrome bike. It was a knockoff that had been painted over to look like the real thing.

It was just another one of those things my mother promised and promised and never came through on. In any case, it got stolen.

This was just normal in our family. It never changed. If I gave my parents money for cigarettes and beer, they always said, "I'll pay you back." Yeah, yeah. Never happened.

Today, when my kids ask for something, we talk about it. They'll always get the everyday stuff, like food and clothes, but when they want something extra, we have a conversation about what they want, talk about if it's reliable and usable, and how they're going to work for it. If that talk goes well, I help them any way I can. If I say I'm going to help, I do. I always follow through.

Giving People What They Want

At 10, I got my first official job, peeling potatoes every day after school at a fish-and-chips shop on the corner of Canon Street and Roslyn. That was my first paycheck. And good thing, too, because I needed the money to feed the washing machine at the laundromat so I could wear clean clothes to school. Many a Saturday saw me hauling my clothes to the laundromat. I made enough money to wash them but not dry them, so I'd have to haul the heavy, wet load back home in a garbage bag and hang them to dry. Or just wear 'em wet.

My father didn't like us kids to use the washer at home. Used up too much electricity, he said, though I noticed he didn't mind using it for his own clothes. Sort of like he kept the TV on 24 hours a day and the air conditioning too. I snuck laundry in once in a while, when he wasn't home, but mostly, I just figured that was the way it was.

I discovered I could do things for people and they'd pay me. Seemed like a sweet deal. By the time I was 11, I was parking cars for people at sports events. I'd find a parking lot that had been closed down, stick up a sign saying "$10 parking," and rake it in. It worked so well, I got friends involved. Four of us covered the streets on all four corners around the stadium, and we split the money at the end of the night, until we were pushed out by the pros.

I didn't rest during the game either. Once the parking lot was full, I'd stand outside the game and ask for tickets. Everyone saw me as the poor kid, not dressed well, who couldn't afford a ticket so they'd give them to me. I'd turn around and sell them.

One day when I was scalping tickets, a man called me on it. "I gave you a ticket for free," he said, "and you sold it!"

"Yeah," I admitted, "Sorry."

"If you wanted to go to the game, you could've sat with me. I would've bought you a hot dog or something."

I told him I sold that ticket for enough money to buy five days of food, and he looked at me like he was going to cry.

I felt bad, but it was true. I needed that money. I never used it for anything bad. I never bought drugs or alcohol. I just spent it on food or let my parents "borrow" it.

School Days, Cruel Days

I discovered pretty early on that I could sell almost anything. Even a garage full of stolen Kraft dinners.

But selling things didn't make me popular at school. When that whole mac and cheese scam went down, the local paper wrote an article about it. Every family in town read that article, so when I went to school the next day I was teased and bullied worse than ever before.

School was tough all around. I had a hard time reading and writing so kids made fun of me for that. The teachers never praised my performance. My family kind of backed me up but the way they did things, it didn't help. My mother would go in and fight with the teachers. My sister too. It wasn't pretty.

I didn't play sports until high school so I didn't have that as a way to fit in. Nobody used the word "bullied" then but that's what I was: Bullied. Every day.

I didn't have the nicest shoes. I never had the cleanest uniform. I was short, fat, and picked on by everyone.

After school, kids beat me up all the time for being different. It was so bad I would take different routes home in the hopes that I could avoid the kids who would beat me up. When I couldn't take the beatings any more, I started working out in the school gym every day. I was going to get strong so they couldn't push me around. Then I learned how to fight. The beatings finally stopped.

I got into my own fights, of course. It was normal. Someone insults you, you don't walk away! You fight! Even when it's two or three of them, you still fight. In fact, it was often two or three of them because bullies are always together.

One day, I had to fight one of the toughest kids in school. By this time, I was a wrestler so I knew what I was doing. We went at it, and I hooked him up and pinned him. The whole gym broke out cheering. I locked that guy up and made him say "mercy." The next day, people called me by name in the hallway. "Roger, how's it going?" They'd never done that before. One kid, a little Chinese guy who was always picked on because he studied all the time, even gave me a hug. He said I gave him faith. The bullies weren't as tough as they thought they were.

Even when the beatings stopped, and I could stay late after school working out or playing football, I always looked over my shoulder. I never trusted anyone and thought any day they could attack me again.

More Than Lunch Money

No such thing as a free lunch, they say. Oh, yeah? In sixth grade, I did better than that. I made money on lunch.

It was obvious to all my teachers that my family didn't have the money for hot lunches and many of them stepped up to help. One of my favorite teachers sent me down the street to Gumbo Sandwich to get his lunch and he gave me two bucks to get my own. Perfect. Then he asked other teachers too. Soon, I had up to 10 teachers sending me with a fistful of dollars to buy lunch. I could buy it all and have money left over. Even better, the sandwich shop got to know me because I was good for business. They started giving me free food. I made a killing. Every day!

At 12, I also started playing football. Of course, my father never came to my games. Except one day. I knew he was in the stands so I played like I was on steroids. I got a fumble recovery and a reception. I almost got another reception but didn't catch it. My coach was thrilled. He told my dad he should come to more games.

You'd think my dad would have congratulated me on the game and told me how proud he was of my performance that day, right? Not my dad. He just complained about the one missed reception. He never said how cool that fumble recovery was or how great my reception was. Not a positive word was said. Even a simple, "Good game" or "That was awesome" would have been nice to hear. Instead, all he said was, "If you could touch it, you could have caught it."

Thanks, Dad.

I played football on and off for seven years and that was the only game he came to.

He didn't go to many events, actually, because he was a chain smoker. He couldn't sit in public not smoking.

My mom came to everything. That should've helped but she got in fights with other parents or anyone who said something she didn't like. Or she'd insult people and start fights with them.

I'm creating a whole different kind of world for my kids. I try not to miss anything. I'm there for my son's football games and my daughter's dance competitions, no matter how packed our schedule is. I am busy and I work hard but my kids take priority. If they need me, a property can wait. I support them and their dreams.

I can't imagine my kids fighting anyone but that was what my dad wanted from us. I'd get in a fight in front of my dad just to make him happy.

One day, some boys threatened my sister. They came to our house. There were two of them so I didn't want to fight. My dad was standing there on the front porch watching me.

"Well, what are you doing?" he asked.

"There's two of them," I said.

"So what?!"

I fought them both. Whipped their asses, even though they were bigger and older than me. Actually got one of them up in the air over our picket fence before my sister and dad yelled at me. Then I just dropped him. That was a scary moment. I could've killed that kid, just to impress my father.

I never stopped trying to impress him. I even fought my sister because he told me to. I'll never forget chasing her to the top of the stairs and punching her in the face. It haunts me. Since that day, I've never stopped protecting her.

The same with my brother. One day, I got him locked up in a sleeping hold and just kept squeezing until he tapped out. He almost passed out. My dad just told him, "You got what you were asking for."

Paid to Fight at 15

Fighting was part of my life, at school and at home. In grade nine, I got into one of the worst fights of my life. There was this kid, Andre, who was a couple of years older than me and part of a powerful group in the neighborhood. He and his friends ran the school. They were tough, and their dads controlled a lot of what went on in town. We didn't talk to them.

I stayed out of their way like everyone else, until the day Andre marched up to me in the cafeteria and tried to butt in line ahead of me. I said no. So he threw my lunch on the floor. I knew who he was but it didn't matter. I went after him. Beat him up.

And then, his brother appeared saying we had to go to the office right away. This should have scared me more than the fight but I was in that office every day. I knew the secretaries by name. It didn't seem like a big deal until I was sitting there with Andre and we heard his father walking down the hall. Click, click, click went his boots. Everyone knew who was wearing those boots. Everyone was scared, from the secretary to the teachers.

We were all freaked out, but when this guy appeared in the office, he just said, "What happened?"

Andre said, "We got in a fight. He gave me a shiner."

The dad looked at me and asked, "Why'd you give my son a shiner?"

"He threw my lunch on the ground," I said.

He wanted to know more. "What do you mean?" he asked.

"Well, I had fries and ketchup and Andre wanted it. He thought he was God, so he grabbed it and threw it on the ground."

His eyes were back on his own kid now. "Did you do that?" he demanded.

Andre said, "Yes, Dad."

I couldn't believe he admitted it. I also couldn't believe the father's reaction. He apologized. To me. And handed me a hundred bucks for my trouble.

I was stunned.

It had never occurred to me not to fight back. My parents said, "Always fight back." If someone looks at you weird, punch him in the face. Plus, I was bullied so much, I was used to having to defend myself. It never stopped and the teachers didn't help. It was always my fault. "What did you do this time, Roger?"

I loved it when I didn't go to school. Some days, when my mom got her paycheck, she'd pull me out of school to go pay bills with her. It was awesome. I didn't have to deal with being picked on in school.

Still, I stayed in school. As far as my parents were concerned, I could've dropped out at any time, but I wanted to make it to 12th grade and graduate. Even if I wanted to drive a bus, I'd need my diploma.

I got there, while working all the time, but I don't recommend that approach. Today, I want my kids to have a very different experience. I don't want them working part time while they are in school because they feel they have to do it to help pay the family bills. I want them to work if they choose to because they want the experience and want some spare spending money for the extra wants in their life. I want them to be able to concentrate on school and sports, not supporting the family. That's enough for them. I do give them a monthly allowance they can use for extras. Or save it. Which they do. They each have built a savings account.

Hot Dog Entrepreneur

When I was 16, I worked at a dollar store for a while and then at a club. For a while I did both, after attending school and participating in sports—5 p.m to 9 p.m. at the dollar store and 9:30 p.m. to 3 a.m. at the club. All night long, I carried drinks and stuff so the waitresses didn't have to and cleaned up after all the fights. You were supposed to be 18 for the busboy job, but I was a big kid so I got away with it. At the end of the night, I got paid in tips.

While I was working at the club, I bought a hot dog cart. First day, parked outside the club, I made 300 bucks. Holy shit! I quit the busboy job and picked up my final paycheck.

Not that I saw any of the money. Here's how it was: My name is Roger Auger. My dad's name is Roger Auger. Care to guess who cashed that check and kept it for himself? That happened to me all the time. Once I turned 18, my father took out credit cards in my name. Once, when

I was 15, he even cosigned a loan for my sister's trailer and convinced the bank he wasn't the signer, I was. Even though 15-year-olds can't sign for loans!

I had terrible credit until I figured out I had to use "Jr." in my name.

Right around 18, I started to see I was making my own way. I didn't have to be anything like my dad. The hot dog cart business was going great. I had carts in different locations, and I bought a car to haul the carts. I built up relationships with suppliers and customers. I had eight locations going at once. Turned out, I was an entrepreneur.

I wasn't a great one yet, though. Still tied to my family, I gave close family members and a few friends jobs. And they stole from me. The hot dog carts handled only cash so it wasn't hard to do, but pretty soon I noticed some locations were selling buns and meat that were so cheap I'd never sell them. Customers complained. My family and friends were buying the cheap stuff and skimming the extra profits.

So many days, I didn't want to get up and go to work in the morning. I was so tired. But I needed the money. I knew there had to be a better way to build a future.

I never wanted a handout—the only reason I did the lunch run when I was 12 was because I knew I was giving something to people in return for their generosity.

I always had a strong work ethic. Still do. I can't stop working even on vacation—if I go somewhere without internet and I can't work, I feel like a loser. Probably because I never got any approval so I kept on trying. My dad would argue over any accomplishment. If I passed an exam, he'd say I'd done the essay question wrong. Didn't matter what it was.

I'm still trying to get to the next level because I know it'll never be enough.

By the time I was 18 or 19, I had seen enough to know I didn't want to follow in my dad's footsteps. I didn't want to be drunk all the time and blame everyone else for my problems.

It came to me that I always had money and they didn't. My mother, my father, my sister, or my brother. They never had a dime. But guess what? They didn't work for it. I did.

If you're a young person reading this, and people have told you you'll never amount to anything, don't listen to them. Find something you love to do and something you're good at. Maybe it isn't the usual stuff, like school and sports. Maybe you have a great singing voice or love to build things. Whatever it is, do that. I was never going to be a hockey star or an incredible student but I was good at selling stuff, and that's what helped me move ahead. Don't worry about what others say you should be. Worry about being something that makes you feel good. Go for your passions.

> If you want to help a kid, it can be as simple as believing in them. Believe that they can do more and be more. And show them if you can.

CHAPTER 6

THE FIRST STEP INTO A NEW LIFE

Once you know the life you are living isn't what you want for yourself or your family, what do you do?

If I tell you to follow your passion but you don't have food on the table every day, that's hard advice to follow, isn't it?

The first step is to believe. From wherever you're sitting, my advice might sound nuts. That could never work! And what does this guy know about it, anyway?

I know a lot about it. You've heard the troubled place I came from, but you probably don't know how far away I got. I got far, far away. Mentally, it's like I went to an entirely different continent. I don't live paycheck to paycheck, running scams. I don't struggle every day, doing drugs and alcohol, and don't work because I have to—but because I want to. But physically, I am still in the same city as my family. I just travel in totally different social circles and live my own life with minimal interactions with them.

Today, I'm a successful businessman with an amazing wife, kids, home, friends, and life.

My hot dog venture eventually was replaced by real estate investing and property management.

I did it by following my dream to be an entrepreneur in real estate, a dream that began when I was very young. I'm an entrepreneur. That's what I am and what I've always been. I could sell sand in the desert.

Standing outside in freezing temperatures selling hotdogs, my mind was always on the end game. I had a bigger plan for why I was doing this. I kept my vision and goals each night I spent standing behind a hot dog cart in my early twenties. I believed my life could be better and that it would be better. And I wasn't going to stop until it was.

It's not about believing that you should get anything handed to you or that anything will come easy. It is about knowing deep in your heart that you can and will *make* the life you deserve. And you will keep going until you do.

Belief Is Not Enough

Belief doesn't pay the bills.

The next step is to know your numbers. You might call this a budget.

You won't create the life you want working a nine-to-five job. You are going to have to do whatever it takes, and it takes more than a single job to get what you are dreaming about.

THE FIRST STEP INTO A NEW LIFE

As I said, I've wanted to be a landlord ever since I was a kid but that didn't happen right away. I also knew it wasn't going to happen with a day job, even a somewhat corporate one, like the one I had once selling phone services for Bell. I was on commission, but even as the top-performing sales person eight years in a row, I wasn't making enough to fulfill my landlord dream on that income alone.

I kept working that first hot dog stand five nights a week. It didn't leave me much time. But I spent any extra time I had thinking about, and planning, the future. I knew how much money I needed to make to survive—to make sure my kids had clothes and my bills were paid.

I don't regret spending all that time working, but I am sorry I missed a lot of family things. In those early times, some days I barely saw my kids, and it wasn't like I could go out to the movies with my wife, Crystal, on a Friday night. I always had to work. I could never take a break because in the hot dog business, you have to keep showing up at the same place night after night. If you don't show up at your location, rain or shine, the people who depend on you being there—club and bar owners who loan you a spot to sell on—will tell you to go somewhere else next time.

I got through it because I knew I didn't want to go back where I came from. I never wanted my kids to go there. They had to have clothes and food on the table. I wanted them to be able to go to the movies. I wanted our family to have cars and keep the bills paid. So I knew my numbers. I had a budget and a plan.

You need to know your numbers. How much money do you need to be making so your bills are paid and you can start to put some money aside for your dream, whatever that is? Maybe you have to go to night school, work a second or third job, or hustle to get into real estate like I did. Whatever your dream is, you have to know how much you need to be making and find a way.

I knew working at Bell wasn't covering it so I kept up with the hot dogs. I worked both jobs until I was in my late thirties. And in 2001, I became a homeowner!

Buying My First House

Our first home was a rental at first. We rented it from Crystal's parents. Our monthly rent was just like making the mortgage payments, so I asked them if I could unofficially buy it from them and work towards the official purchase over time. With my two jobs and Crystal's work at a daycare center, it could work.

We saved as much as we possibly could so we had a down payment. I think we had pulled together about $25,000. With that much in the bank, I figured there had to be a bank that would give us a mortgage to buy the house so I started shopping around.

None of the major banks would finance our purchase, but finally I got a credit union to say yes. And finally it began. I owned my first house. We officially bought it from Crystal's parents and I could see a way to get into real estate investing.

The thing is, I know how hard it was to save our down payment for our house. I knew that saving $50,000-$100,000 to buy rental properties was going to be too difficult to do in any reasonable amount of time so I started with my own home. I was patient and focused. I used the income I was making from the hot dog stand to pay down the mortgage on my house twice as fast.

We found another house. My wife, Crystal, fell in love with the property so we put in a lowball offer. The negotiations went back and forth quite a bit, but we actually ended up getting the property.

It was a power of sale, which works like this: **The mortgagee is selling the property to repay the mortgage debt.** These can be good deals because the seller is desperate to get the money. But it isn't always a deal and you still have to know what you're buying.

We loved the property, but financing it wasn't easy. The only way this was going to work was if we sold our current home. Then the credit union would give us what is called a bridge loan. In other words, the bank offers financing as a bridge to go from one property to the other but it has a condition on it. In this case, the condition was that we sell our home.

Unfortunately, or maybe it was fortunately, our home didn't sell.

This meant the mortgage from the credit union wouldn't happen because it was conditional on our home selling. So I had to find other financing. I ended up finding financing through another bank. We rented our home out and we moved into the new property.

That's when I could begin to call myself a landlord. To get my next property, I got a line of credit. I purchased it, because I knew that the expenses on the property including the mortgage were going to be lower than the rent I would be able to collect every month from the property. It was a moneymaker. I secured this property and the line of credit without talking to Crystal about it.

I didn't even have her permission to do the deal.

I don't recommend making big investments or purchases without consent and discussion with your spouse. My wife handled this well, but I was lucky. The deal was excellent and I was very confident, but many wives would have not handled that as well as my amazing wife. Crystal believes in me and fully supports me so it was okay. But that could be a big problem for some.

When there was enough equity in that property and our old home, I refinanced and bought two more from a person who wanted out of the rental property business. It worked out really well for me; they were tired of dealing with the hassles and I was so excited to get into the business that I solved their problem while scoring my next two rentals. Now I was really in business with four rental properties total.

I realized that each new unit I rented out meant fewer hours selling hot dogs, so I pushed hard to get those first properties. And I worked on the real estate business at the same time as everything else.

But I knew my numbers. And in the first year of holding a property, I knew the only way to make it work for me was to pay double the amount of the mortgage payment to the bank each month. Instead of paying a mortgage payment of $1,200, for example, I would pay $2,400 to pay down the mortgage and build equity so I could refinance and buy my next property in a year. But to make that work, I needed income so I kept up both jobs—until I was passed over for a promotion at Bell. That was the end of it for me.

I always exceeded my numbers there—if they said I had to make $10, I made $20. My performance should have been rewarded but I got nothing over my commission. Something about that didn't make sense. I noticed my manager was driving a BMW, while I drove a beat-up 4x4. And I was working a lot more then she was! Then I found out that the managers got bonuses based on staff performance. The staff didn't get bonuses.

The company only cared about themselves and their management, not about their hard-working, performing employees. They even cut commissions, so we'd have to work harder and longer and make less money for our efforts.

I wanted out. After eight years of investing, real estate could give me the exit I wanted.

The third step is to create multiple streams of income so you can pay your bills, save, and then invest the money.

Multiple streams of income are the key. Nobody I know who is successful today relies on one source of income. You can't count on a job to pay you forever, and you can't expect that a business that is booming today will always be booming. You need options.

Real estate was my dream. And it's something that anybody can do. You don't need special training or any kind of education to become a real estate investor. If you want to be a realtor or a mortgage broker helping other people with their real estate deals, then you need to invest in a lot of training for the license, but to be an investor, you can start today.

Of course, you're taking some big risks if you start investing without educating yourself. There are things you need to learn like what makes a good deal, how to run the numbers, what renovations make financial sense, and how you're going to attract tenants. There are risks you have to take but working as a real estate investor is something that is possible for anybody. There are no prerequisites for you to start or enter.

I'm not saying you need to invest in real estate. That is just what worked for me but it was always my dream. I just want you to go for whatever it is you're dreaming about.

But if real estate is your dream, too, know that you will likely need more income to do it. For years, this was me holding many jobs. Then it was me with a day job and the hot dog stands at night. Eventually, I was adding rental properties to the mix.

THE FIRST STEP INTO A NEW LIFE

Rental properties are what finally allowed me to ease away from the hot dog stands.

The first two rental properties brought in $1,000 per month in cashflow. That allowed me to work fewer nights at the hot dog stand. Of course, I was now spending my time working on real estate, but it was better than standing outside selling hot dogs.

As I added more rental property income I went from working on the hot dog stands five days a week to four, then three, and so on. Eventually, I had just one staff member, and when he went off to a full-time job, I was making enough on rentals that I didn't have to do it anymore. I parked the cart for good. (In one of the next chapters I'll share my real estate investing strategy with you, but know that there are many ways to invest in real estate. I'm just going to share the one that has worked for me.)

But rentals aren't always enough to pay the bills. It's good to have other sources of income too. Sometimes opportunities come up that will allow you to do this. For me, another source of income has been property management. This means I manage other people's properties and get paid a percentage of their rental income every month for taking care of finding tenants and overseeing the operations of their properties.

I wasn't exactly planning on being a property manager. One of the neighboring owners of a rental property found me cutting grass at one of my properties nearby and asked if I mowed lawns. I told him that this was my rental property and that I was just there managing it and doing some work to keep it looking good.

This really caught his attention because he was unhappy with how his rental on the same street was going. He had problems with his tenants and asked me if I would help with that. I helped him, and then he hired me to manage his property full time.

I realized this was a great source of cashflow for doing something that I am actually pretty good at. Remember, I can sell stolen Kraft dinners so handling tenant troubles is not that hard for me. So I figured that this was an opportunity. I put an ad up and got a bunch more property-manager clients.

The ads generated a lot of new business, then word-of-mouth really started to kick in. I started to get referrals from local realtors and investment groups.

When I got the first check from my tenants, I knew I was onto something: Fees from managing properties can really add up to create a strong income source. It also allows me to not stress about the cashflow on the first year of a rental property.

I'll talk about why that's important shortly.

The fourth, and final, step is to keep pursuing growth.

I think I can retire when I'm 50 but I'm not sure I'll want to.

I want my kids to have an easier start than I had. I also want to enjoy retirement. I know too many people who are struggling after retirement. They're making ends meet but that's all. I don't want to be like that. I've been there, and I'm not going back! So I'm not going to rest comfortably just because my bills are paid today. And you shouldn't either. Things can change. Just because you have money today doesn't mean it will be there tomorrow if you're not smart about it.

I do define success differently than I did once. Today, my success is my kids doing well in school and sports.

But I like working. I happily get up at six every morning to get to work. I get excited about building my real estate business and I look forward to the work ahead.

I have 14 properties now. That should be enough. Yet I'm in the middle of a restructuring that will create another income stream and a third company. The new venture will have me buying, renovating, and selling houses pretty quickly. I really don't ever stop. And I don't know if I want to.

I like working and building my business. The important thing for me is knowing I'm in control of my life. I don't have someone telling me what I can and can't do. If I want to buy a new watch, I buy a new watch. If my kids need something, I can get it for them, no questions asked. I'm not worrying about the next paycheck.

My daily life is nothing like it was growing up. I go to the gym every morning and answer a hundred emails and text messages the moment I get into work at a property management company. Then it's off to deal with contractors, tenants, inspections, and new properties. As a kid, I spent a lot of time alone but no more. On a regular day, I meet with real estate agents and clients all day long. I might have a lunch date with one client and a dinner date with 30 clients and that's on days when I don't meet with the Abundance Group, a bunch of investor friends.

But none of this happens unless I'm growing as a person. And that is the fourth and important step. You have to pursue growth. Challenge yourself. Find people who will help you be the best version of yourself. And take care of yourself. My schedule is very busy, but I begin most days by going to the gym. Taking care of myself is my first priority.

If you're scared to do something, find someone who is doing it and try to learn how they did it. Chances are, they were scared when they started out too. Ask a lot of questions of everyone around you. I learn from everyone in my life. I grow every day that I spend time with people, from my investor friends to my clients and agents. They offer other perspectives. That's important.

I guess there is a step five, and that is to take a chance on the things you have passion for.

Nobody owes you anything, so if you're sitting around waiting for someone to give you a chance, give you a raise, or do anything, you're wasting your time.

The only way you are going to get anywhere in life and enjoy your life is if you pursue the things you are passionate about. And I firmly believe if you work hard enough and have enough passion, the money follows. I've seen it:

a lot of people hire me because I'm so passionate about real estate.

Passion is more powerful than you probably realize.

CHAPTER 7
HANDLING THE HATERS

When I started dating my wife, my uncle thought she was out of my league. He told me, "You need to learn how life is. You're going to be a bum."

More than 20 years later, he's still on disability and hasn't done anything different with his life.

I didn't listen to him. I didn't listen to any of the haters. You shouldn't either. The haters don't tell you what they think about *you*. They are telling you what they think about themselves. My uncle was really looking at me with his only filter on life. It was a filter that says, "Look, I'm a bum, and will always be a bum." He doesn't expect anything more out of himself, so he doesn't expect anything more out of anyone else either.

There will always be haters. And the worst part is that many of them are the people who appear in your life every single day. Growing up, my friends and family were the biggest haters. They didn't encourage me to become a landlord, work two jobs, or do anything, really. When I told them I wanted to have rentals, they said things like, "Tenants will trash the house," "You'll get bums who won't pay rent for a year," or "It's nothing but a hassle to have rentals."

You'd think haters go away as you succeed but they don't. When I was working my hot dog stands, I remember a girlfriend I had whose parents told her to dump me because they didn't want to see her on welfare. Now that I'm a successful real estate businessman, people can't say things like that about me. But there are still haters. Now there are people who are jealous of my success. People who want me to fail like they are failing so they say negative things. They say bad things about me. Others will turn their nose up at how I invest in real estate, pointing out all the problems and risks with what I am doing.

People are going to hate. It will often feel like there are more haters than helpers. Keep going. You are the only one who can lift yourself up. You have to do this with what you believe about yourself. I actually think that people are more vocal about being haters than they are about being positive. I know that everyone has an opinion about what you are doing. If you own property, people might call you a slumlord. Some tenants that I tried to help ended up not paying rent for five months and still slammed me all over the internet. After five months of letting them live rent free, I had to evict them.

I gave them a few chances to start paying me before I did that. I was nicer than most landlords and still I get a lot of hate. Another of my tenants was mad at me after

I'd evicted him. He created 18 different email addresses so he could post 18 different negative reviews about my company on Google. I had to pull my business page off of Google because an online search for me would turn up these negative reviews first.

It's not fair. And who will people believe in many situations—the "rich landlord" or the "poor tenant?"

So I took down my Twitter and Facebook pages and went on. There will be haters. I know I gave these people more chances than I should have, but I believed that they needed a break and I wanted to help them.

My family is full of haters. They rarely say nice things that show me any sort of support. I stopped looking there. In fact, I try to avoid any conversations at all that trigger any sort of negative talk about what I do. It doesn't always work but I try.

Here's how I handle the haters and what I recommend you do:

Believe in yourself. If you don't give up, then you will succeed. So believe in that even if nobody else will. Don't accept what they say. Instead, visualize yourself succeeding.

Get away from the haters. They are jackasses. This can be hard when the biggest haters are in your family (and they often are). But you must see them less. And when you do have to see them, prepare yourself. I see my family as little as possible, and when I have to, I prepare by reminding myself of the things they will say and to not provoke them. It's easier to agree with them (even when you don't) or avoid the conversations that trigger the negative talk. It's hard and I'm always exhausted after but you have to protect yourself. Put up guards, prepare yourself, and remind yourself what you have done and all that you can do.

Remind yourself of your accomplishments and keep track so you keep going. I carry around a notebook most of the time. This notebook has quotes, achievements, and notes to myself. I also write down every single house I buy (14 so far!), what I paid for them, and what they are worth now. It helps me remember what I am capable of and reduces the impact of the haters.

Surround yourself with great people. For me, this is my Abundance Group. I'll tell you about them and how you can find your own next.

Find Your Abundance Group

The fact that I am a part of a group of people who call themselves the Abundance Group says a lot about how different my life is now. This group focuses on the positive. For one thing, we have a lot of fun. We went to Vegas one month. Next, we're going to drive exotic cars—Ferraris—around Niagara Falls for three hours before dinner and virtual golf.

I never played as a kid. I heard about other kids going to Chuck E. Cheese and places like it, but I was more concerned about making money than anything else. If I went anywhere for dinner, it was the food bank. So, it's even more special and fun to play as an adult. Now

I'm feeding my soul, not just my pocketbook, and that is changing my life.

Find ways to feed your soul. I do that with the friends I surround myself with and by giving back. Little charity things, not just giving tenants a chance to pay late rent for months at a time (although that is certainly one way). I'll tell you more in a minute. First, more about the Abundance Group because I hope you find a group like this too.

The other members of this group are more like my first girlfriend's family. They grew up in nice houses. They all have university degrees. I'm the only one who grew up with drunk, drug-addicted parents and didn't go to college. I'm still shocked sometimes listening to them talk about money, cars, and restaurants. I wonder, how the hell did I get in this group?

I mean, the conversations they have floor me sometimes. My "old friends" always talked about how their boss was an asshole and they only made $45,000 for doing someone else's crappy work. It was about where we were going to go drinking, who was fighting with who, and how crappy work was. Sometimes they would talk about their dream of making $100,000 a year, like if they did that they would be super rich. But that was always followed with laughs because it was impossible. I just sat there listening, like I always do. They were so excited about 45 or 50 grand a year and I get it. I really do. I understand why they were happy to think about retiring at 65 or 70 years old. But that's not how I look at it anymore.

I feel out of place with the old gang, even though we share a history and I do feel loyal to them. I wasn't getting any smarter hanging out with them, though.

Now I'm in on conversations about stocks and bonds, leadership, education, and self-motivation. With these Abundance Group guys, I'm talking about how to save money for our kids' college tuitions or how to invest for retirement. We also talk about how we're going to give back. We do some pretty soul-fulfilling work at Thanksgiving and Christmas feeding families , and a Basket Brigade for Easter.

I'm definitely learning so much from our local Abundance Group, which we call "Hambundance" because we're all based in Hamilton, Ontario, Canada. But the truth is, I feel a little out of place with this new gang too. I like hanging out with Hambundance, but we have different upbringings. We don't share history, but we do share similar visions for the future. We talk about retiring early, spending quality time with our kids, and things that are important to me and my future.

But sometimes it feels like they have so much money they don't have to think about money.

When we were talking about going to Vegas, it felt like each guy was just able to say, "Yes, let's go." For me, I was wondering if I can afford it. I had to think about how to pay for it, even though I could pay for it easily. There is always a part of me that worries whether I should spend money or not, just in case. Maybe these guys have those kinds of thoughts too. Maybe they also fear not having enough money but it's probably still different. I came from nothing and really know what it's like to have absolutely no money and no backup plans. In my eyes, I'm not at their level yet.

I've been in a few situations where both groups of friends are in the same social situation. For example, when my kids have a birthday party and we have people over. That's what people mean when they say, "My worlds collided." Not that they clash and fight or anything like that, but after introductions and some friendly small chat, the groups separate and segregate. They hang out on their own sides of the room and don't intermingle. It makes sense. But it always leaves me feeling a little weird.

Surround Yourself with Like-Minded People

The best way to handle the haters is to create your own Abundance Group. It's not about making money, it's about making life better. A product of making life better is that we make more money, but it's not like a typical networking group where so many people show up and figure out how they can take from others. It's a group where we figure out how we can give. And we talk more about how we can be better as people than being better in business.

But I know if you were telling me about this group 10 years ago, I would have laughed at you. "Where will I find those kind of people? My friends are all living paycheck to paycheck and getting excited about Sunday football, not investment planning or retirement dreams."

In some ways, I feel like I lucked into the Abundance Group. I met some people with whom I just clicked.

There's this one realtor in my area, Erwin Szeto, who really likes to bring people together. He would invite folks to do different things and host events. As I attended those, it became fairly clear who had common interests and got along. That's our Abundance Group.

Maybe you aren't lucky enough to have that organizer friend like I had to help me find this amazing group I spend time with. So here's what I would do to create the group all over again.

Find People Who Like what You Like.

Part of that might be finding people who do what you do. If I was an electrician I would find people in the same trade as me and ask them what they like to do. A big part of this group is that we do fun things together. So you need to like to do similar things. And having a shared career path helps. We are all investors in our group. Plus, giving back to our community is really important to each of us.

Maybe you don't know if you will enjoy the same things at first so just start by inviting a few people out to do one thing you like to do. Maybe that is a game of golf or a hike.

Now if you aren't sure where to find these people, maybe you can check association meetings for your industry, or think about who you went to trade school with or attended some other training with, or look at the sporting events you like to attend and find other sports team fans.

I think the best way to find these kind of people, though, is going to like-minded events. So if you're into learning entrepreneurial ideas or real estate investing, you're probably going to find people you'll want to hang out with at these kinds of events.

Who are you looking for?

Of course, you need to make your own list, but in my mind the most important traits of each member are the following things:

- Positivity. If someone always sees things as bad or negative, it's not a good idea to have them in your group.

- Uplifting. Will this person lift you and the others up on a bad day? It's not about being fake happy or anything like that but how do they see the world? Are they looking to make it better, and do they see good in people?

- Self-learning. A key component to a group like this is that everyone in the group is pursuing more knowledge and is happy to share the knowledge they are learning. They have to want to learn or teach.

- Similar interests. Fun is so important and a part of what bonds us in this group, so if the people in the group don't like to do the same things as you, then it's not going to work in the long run.

- Goal-oriented. We set goals for each other in the group and hold each other accountable to the goals.

The most important thing is that you surround yourself with people who are going to elevate you in life. Again, the focus is not on elevating you in business. Business comes second. It's not about using each other to get business. It's for having fun and learning. Lifting each other up lifts yourself but that's not why you're doing it. It's not about getting high enough so you drop them. These are going to be lifelong friends, so choose carefully—you want to grow with them.

A Final Note on Passion

My passion for real estate happened at a young age and it never faded. That doesn't happen for everyone. Especially if you aren't exposed to a lot of different things. So try things. If a friend suggests you go see a play or visit his uncle at his car dealership, don't dismiss it. Go. See if you like it or if something interests you. Do that until you find something that you get really excited about and the excitement doesn't fade. That's when you know you've found something that you're passionate about that is worth focusing on for your life and surrounding yourself with people like you to grow around that passion and share it with.

We're about to get deeper into my passion, real estate, but I'm not assuming or suggesting that real estate should be your passion. It can be a tool you use to get more financial resources in your life to fund your passion, if you want to do that. Or it can just be an idea you use to ensure you chase after the thing you do care about. But you first have to try a lot of things so you know what you are passionate about.

CHAPTER 8

BUILDING EQUITY AND CASHFLOW WITH REAL ESTATE

There are hundreds of books out there that will teach you how to invest in real estate. There are dozens of strategies for investing in real estate and making money doing it. It's like football. There are 12 different people on the team doing 12 very different things but they all win the game.

So what I want to share with you isn't *the* way to invest in real estate. But it's how I have done it and what works for me. It's one strategy of many. I didn't learn from anybody. I taught myself. I owned eight properties before I joined my first real estate investing club (Rock Star Real Estate group, run by Nick and Tom Karadza).

Joining the group has been great for me but I already had my own strategy in place by the time I joined them. And that leads me to the first point I want to share with you. Don't listen to what other people say. Figure out what works for you. Do your own work. Find your own market areas. You are the only one who can really know what is right for you so put in the effort and figure it out.

That said, you might not have any idea how to start. Here's my advice:

1. **Know your area.**

    My first property was in the area where I'd gone to college. The entire time I was a student paying rent, I was calculating what I was paying my landlord, how much he was making, and what his mortgage probably was. I knew how much money he was making. I also knew what kind of properties were in demand in that area and what wasn't valued as high as it should be.

    I knew the area because I had lived in it. I talked to a lot of people too. I asked realtors, my landlord, and other people questions. I knew what students thought about different features and streets.

    You need to know the area personally. If you haven't lived there, figure out what you can do to get to know an area better. Spend time there. Ask people lots of different questions. Look at houses. Don't rely on a realtor or anyone else to tell you if an area is good or not. Know it yourself. Figure out what you think!

    When I look at areas, I figure out who the tenants are most likely to be. And I make sure I'll have options. I don't want to get stuck with a property if the market changes a bit.

Case Study: Knowing the Area Pays Off

I found this property that was $255,000 in the area I went to school. It wasn't the best property because it was set up for a student rental and it was beat up. And the area wasn't going to be that strong for student rentals for that long.

If I was to rate it on a scale of 1 to 10 for all the factors, I would say it was a 5 out of 10. It was already run down as a student rental. It would secure cash flow as a student rental but I knew it could do more as a duplex. The problem was that I didn't have the money to turn it into a duplex. I barely had the money for the down payment. But I knew the area was poised for growth and that this property would be okay as a student rental for a while. I could be patient.

There were lots of things that made the area great, like the fact that it was near a major college, had easy access to all the downtown amenities, and was only a seven-minute drive from the highway. But the reason I knew it was going to grow was the level of investment happening in the area. A hospital was being built, which would bring in a lot of jobs. The college was expanding, which would bring in jobs and students, and Walmart was buying a bunch of property around it to create a super center. If Walmart is investing big money in an area, it's good to pay attention to what they might be seeing that you're not.

Normally, I do whatever I can to force the appreciation and pay the property down fast but this property was a little rough. It wasn't adding equity very fast. I had to wait longer for the equity to build up.

After five years, I was able to get a second mortgage on the property for $100,000. The cost to turn it into a duplex was roughly $75,000. That money was enough to do the renovation and pay the mortgage fees while I renovated. Once I was done with the renovations, I refinanced, and now it brings in $3,400/month in rent and $1,200 of that is positive cashflow.

Now that the work is done, the property was just appraised at $540,000.

If students come back to the area, I can turn it back into a student rental but in the meantime it's generating more rent as a duplex. I knew that this property would have this option when I bought it because I did my research. I actually expected the student rental market to dry up at some point. I looked at what was available on the market. I talked to people and asked what people were looking for but couldn't find and made sure I wasn't buying in an area where only one type of rental property would work.

2. **Force the Appreciation**

   Force the appreciation on the property and build the equity as fast as you can. Once I buy a property I renovate it so that it's worth more and can get higher rents. When I renovate, I might be turning a single-family home into a duplex. I could be making that same single-family home into a student rental or adding an in-law suite to it. My decision is based on the area and how I will generate the highest rents.

I always make sure I get more than expected rent by adding more rental space or taking advantage of some opportunity. If a property doesn't have the opportunity to do this, I don't buy it. You have to do your homework and learn the area. Then when you buy the property, you have to be smart enough to spot the opportunities. I'll tell you about one I spotted that was on an investor tour we took. Nobody on that tour thought it was a good deal, but I could see something that nobody else spotted.

It's worth mentioning that you can spend a lot of money renovating properties, but not all renovations actually pay off with higher value and higher rents. Every area might be different to a point, but I focus on fixing up kitchens, bathrooms, and flooring on the inside. These will make a big difference in the value for renters and future buyers too! On the outside, I always invest in renovating the landscape—curb appeal, as they say.

That's forced appreciation.

3. **Build equity as fast as you can.**

   Forced appreciation is building equity, but that isn't the only way to grow the equity you have in a property. I do something that very few real estate investors or real estate gurus recommend. I make mortgage payments biweekly and set the amortization at 20-25 years to pay down the mortgage faster.

This approach is very different than many investors because most people really want to make a lot more cashflow on their property. If you want more cashflow, you're not going to want to make your mortgage payments so big, which is what this does. But my goal is not cashflow at this point. I want to get as much equity in this property as possible so I can use that equity to get my next property. That leads in to the fourth and final piece of advice I have on this.

4. **Hold that property for a year, refinance, and buy the next one.**

    If you've been successful in adding a lot of value and paying down the mortgage on your property over the year that has passed, you should be able to refinance to get a better interest rate and pull out the equity to get the down payment to buy the next property.

    Now if you have ever tried to get a mortgage from a bank, or you've done any reading in the real estate space, you may be wondering how I finance these properties with the bank. Banks don't like real estate investors very much. Banks also don't like risk. But I just keep asking.

In Canada, lenders are organized into three tiers. There's A lenders—and this is the top six major banks—BMO, CIBC, National Bank of Canada, Scotiabank, RBC, and TD. They have high standards to get loans. B lenders are banks outside of the big six and have lower barriers to getting loans. C lenders are private money/unregulated lenders.

Many investors focus on getting the lowest possible interest rate so they have to get an A lender to finance their property. This can mean relying on a joint venture partner who has a job so the bank doesn't see them as high risk. Or it can mean waiting until you have a lot of equity and income in your business before approaching an A lending bank on a new investment. For me, my focus is on getting the property because once you own it, the financing is much easier to get later on.

That's not easy. You need to know that going in. Unless you have a really great job, high credit, and a lot of money to begin with, banks aren't going to be super excited to work with you. But I always find financing, and you can too.

How do I finance my properties? I keep asking. And I'll pay 5 percent or even 9 percent on a mortgage to get started.

Starting with A lenders, moving to B and C lenders. I work with private lenders. Again, I believe in myself so I just keep going until I get it done.

The cashflow at the start isn't as important to me as buying an appreciating asset. As long as my mortgage cost is covered, then I am good.

Then I repeat the above, renovate, rent out, hold for a year, and refinance.

My best advice to you is to always have a way out. All my properties have three options so I can do more than one thing with them. Every property can be a duplex, a home with an in-law suite, or a single-family home. If the area is good for it, I can also make the property a student rental.

You have to be able to adapt.

Get Good at Seeing What Others Don't

I'm part of a few investment groups now. Sometimes realtors will put together investor tours and take a group of investors around to a bunch of properties that are for sale in their area. I go on these tours sometimes. It's a great way to chat with other investors and learn different approaches. And sometimes you might get to see a property that has a good opportunity.

This happened recently. We were touring a property that was listed for $399,000. It was a two-bedroom house. As a two-bedroom house you'd be lucky to get more than $1,500 rent for it.

The investors in the group all thought this property was crap and overpriced. They knew it could never come close to generating cashflow in its current condition. They were right, but I wasn't looking at what the property was today, I was thinking about what the property could be. And clearly there was the potential to add a suite to this property. So it had duplex potential.

I also explored the attic, as I always do. It had a drop-down ladder. I climbed up there. Other investors were too scared to go up there. The realtor hosting the tour gave me shit for doing that, but what I saw got me really excited about the property. I noticed the ceilings were really high—they were seven feet tall. That got me excited because I could see how two bedrooms could be added up there, making it a four-bedroom house.

I told the other investors on the tour what I had found but the brand-new investors on the tour all said, "Well it's like that for a reason. An attic space is an attic space for a reason," or "But you'd have to build stairs up there and how can you do that?" There were a few experienced real estate investors on the tour as well, but they said that adding those two bedrooms upstairs would take too much money.

It was listed for $399,000—way too high. But I watched the property as the price was lowered a couple of times. When the price dropped to $359,000, I made an offer and ended up buying the property for $355,000.

I added those two bedrooms to the attic, which made for an additional two-bedroom suite on the property.

When the work was done, we were getting:

$1,700 for the upstairs

$1,500 for the suite

$300 for the garage

This property that nobody else could see the potential in now rents for $3,500 per month, more than twice what the two-bedroom would have gone for.

You may hear people telling you that it's not a good time to buy, or that risks are too high to invest in real estate, but I think that you have to be smart about it. Do your research and work hard to uncover the deals that others are overlooking. It would have been so easy to listen to all the other seasoned investors on that tour and go, "Yeah, you're right—that will never work," but I looked at it with my own critical eye to make sure that I was not missing anything. The same goes if everyone is telling you it's a great deal. That's not always true either. You have to do your own work and research.

Jump in, don't over analyze: a mini case study:

One of my joint venture partners missed out on a really great deal because of over analysis. He took a look at the numbers and decided that there wasn't enough cashflow. But he only looked at the first year. He wasn't looking at the bigger picture or the potential. Another partner stepped up to buy in with me, and here's what we did.

We purchased the property for $325,000 (20 percent down, and a mortgage for $290,000). We added $80,000 to renovate the property into a duplex. That just means we added a second unit to the property for rental. When that was done we expected to net about $300/month in cashflow. The first partner said that wasn't enough because he only wanted to invest in properties that would have more than $1,000/month in cashflow.

He was overanalyzing the short term and missing the long term, though.

I looked at it as that was the first year. I've already shared that I don't expect to make money in the first year. My investment approach is not about a one-year plan. The positives of this opportunity far outweighed the negatives.

I guess it's worth noting that I also look at everything with the thought that I started from nothing so I can always rebuild. People who have always had something always feel like they have a lot to lose. If you have started from the bottom and scraped your way to success, you know you can do it again and again, so risks aren't as scary, maybe. This guy was looking at what he could lose if things didn't turn out and wanted a higher margin of cashflow to cover the possible downsides. My focus isn't on what I can lose in a deal like some people. You have to look at the risk but if the positives outweigh the negatives, act!

This deal turned out to be amazing! When we were done with the renovation we refinanced the property. The bank valued it at $550,000 and gave us a mortgage for $440,000!

So we now have a property that we have no money in! In fact, we were reimbursed $150,000 (we'd spent $145,000) because the new mortgage is that much higher than what we had put into the property already! Plus, the existing tenants moved out and we rented it out for much higher rent, so we are now getting $950/month in cashflow from the property that we have no money in with $110,000 equity.

The guy who overanalyzed this missed out because he was focusing on a few negatives that were outweighed by the positive.

Opportunities are everywhere—if people know you're looking.

My son and daughter are active in sports. As I have said, being there for their events is important to me, so I volunteer coach, manage equipment, or buy food for the team. Or I'll run the BBQ at events. I'm very visible as a result. My kids are also good athletes. People know our last name.

A guy had a property near a large university and medical complex that was on the market for a year and a half. He knew me from these sporting events and knew I was a real estate investor so he talked to me about it. It was a house with a cottage behind it.

It wasn't selling because nobody could get financing for it. With two different houses on one property, the banks couldn't figure out how to finance it. He was renting it as a triplex but it was getting super low rent. So even investors who may have been interested couldn't get financing and the numbers on it weren't very strong anyway. It was only getting $3,400 in rent.

He wanted $500,000 for the property. I agreed to purchase it from him for $490,000. The problem for me was the same as the others who had looked at the property, though. I couldn't get this purchase financed either.

Instead, I talked with him about a way to solve the problem. I got a vendor take-back loan (a VTB; the seller acts as the bank for the financing) from him for two years. I put 20 percent down, which was enough for him to pay off the existing financing he had on the property. Because I had a good reputation, he was willing to finance and gave us an interest rate of five percent.

I purchased with a partner because this required some cash for the down payment and the renovation.

The first thing I did was evict two of the tenants. They were bad and should have been gone already! I kept the upper tenants. And I found a way to solve the problem that was stumping the banks. I attached the two properties with a roof so now it's one house.

The city gave us permits for it so it's fully legal. This is the rent we're getting for each of the three units now:

$2,200

$1,500

$1,500

So now we're getting $5,200/month in rent, and when we refinanced the property, the new value was $700,000.

We were able to pay off that VTB after just one year, and now it's a legal triplex, not a single-family home with a cottage.

A deal like this only happened because I'm active in my community and I spent a lot of time trying to figure out how I could solve this problem. I called my insurance company to see what they would allow. I spent time at the city talking about what could be done on that property. I spoke with different banks to understand why financing was such a challenge and what would make the property financeable. In the end, that is how I found this solution.

Real estate has been good to me. I love it. Every property is different. There are always problems to be solved and often it's the person who can see solutions that are outside the box who can really reap the rewards.

You have to love what you're doing and be willing and able to come up with different scenarios for different properties. The big thing to know is that you always have to work on it. You're not just going to be able to coast and do the same thing over and over.

Lots of people have lost their shirts in real estate, and I can see how that can happen if you just follow what other people tell you all the time. Ask a lot of questions and work hard. Know your market and solve other people's problems.

That's really a winning long-term formula.

CHAPTER 9
HELP OTHERS—FEED YOUR SOUL

My son came home from school when he was younger. He'd been pantsed. The kids at school were bullying him.

Now the good thing is that he has a good home life so he knew he was being bullied. But hearing about it brought up a ton of emotions for me. As a kid I was bullied until I had a growth spurt and got bigger than the other kids. But I didn't even realize I was being bullied because that is how I was treated at home. It was just normal to me.

But when it happened to my son, I was furious. It triggered so many strong emotions for me that I wanted to respond more strongly than a parent should. And overreactions can happen so easily for me. I respond with extreme defensiveness in so many situations. If a tenant takes me to small claims court, I defend and escalate the situation with rapid speed. An employee threatened action against me and I immediately fired her. When a contractor threatens me by saying something like, "If you won't do x, I won't show up to the work site," and I respond with, "Fine—don't show up because you don't work for me anymore."

But these tools I learned as a child don't serve me as an adult and entrepreneur, and certainly don't help as a parent. It's not a legacy I want to give to my son either. Not everything can be handled with a F-U attitude and I struggle to do better, to put down the phone, take some perspective, and come up with a different solution. So I waited 24 hours, then I went into the school and met with the principal. The bullying calmed down after that, and part of that was due to *me* being calm.

Being bullied never fully goes away, but you can still succeed. You need self-awareness to try to understand why you are reacting in the ways that you do. And you can help others along the way, especially if you know they deserve a chance. Because some people have just never had anyone give them an opportunity.

I understand both sides of the coin. That's why I do my best to give to those who need help. A big part of that has been the Hamilton Basket Brigade I've been helping to run for several years. I know how much it costs for a family to put together a holiday dinner. It's a lot, especially when you're already stretched thin buying regular groceries. With the Basket Brigade, we find families who could use a free turkey dinner at Easter or Thanksgiving and we provide it to them. The first year, we gave meals to 32 families. There was a huge need, though, so we worked with friends and clients to raise more money. Last year, we served around 350 families. We have dropped off turkey dinners, all fresh food, for four years.

This year, we're changing the program a little. We're serving a smaller number of families but we're having more of an impact than just turkey dinner. Each family sends us a wish list, up to $100 per family member, and we get the items on the wish list for them. A family of five can get $500 worth of stuff to help make it through the year. We buy lots of jackets, boots, winter jackets, ski pants, and toques (that's Canadian for a beanie or winter hat). Other people ask for light bulbs, toiletries, and cleaning supplies. We buy the biggest packages we can find so the gift can last the family all year. We also throw in $100 for food. It helps so much.

When we deliver, it's chaos! The kids are so excited they scream and jump up and down, trying everything on. They're so happy to have a new winter jacket. It brings me back to my childhood because I either wore my brother's old jacket or three layers of sweaters. These kids, even the youngest, get brand new, warm gear for winter. It's a small impact but it's huge for these kids.

We are serving 20 families right now. We'll do it again at Christmas, and one family has 11 kids. That's a lot of boots!

Giving Doesn't Have to Be Big

A few times a week, I buy people's orders in the drive through behind me. I don't do it every time, but a few times a week, I'll pay for the order of the person behind me. It's a little thing, but I always hope they pay it forward. And it makes me feel good to do it too.

The Basket Brigade is something big I do to give back, but you don't have to do something as organized and big as that to make a difference in someone's life.

As a landlord, I will give tenants a chance. Some people have terrible credit or fall on hard times. Nobody would rent to someone like that, but I do. Sometimes people just need someone to believe in them. If a tenant can't make their rent payment one month, I don't just throw them out. I'm not saying this a good business practice. People in my Abundance Group say that I shouldn't do this so much. But I want to help.

I hire anyone who needs a job. I find them work. I even offered this to two of my tenants recently. They are young and didn't have jobs. They like to build things so I figured I could find work for them renovating. They turned me down. "Oh, I have a sore back," one said to me. He's 17! Tell me he didn't learn that behavior from his dad. Better to complain about being "disabled" and expect others to hand things to you than to put in a hard day of work to earn your money.

To tell you the honest truth, I give 10 people a chance and probably only two people really work out. And by work out I don't mean they make me a profit. I mean they come through and pay me rent or work hard and do the thing they should do. But I won't stop helping because if I can help those two people who needed a chance, it's worth it.

One of my best contractors, the guy I can count on to handle a problem in the middle of the night, is someone I took a chance on. His wife got sick and he had to close his business to take care of her. He would have had to file for bankruptcy if I hadn't helped him with some of his payments. Now he's one of my best team members. One upside of doing good things is that it can create really deep loyalty.

I believe it's not always about feeding your pocketbook. Feed your soul and your pocketbook will be filled.

Do things you want to do because it's the better thing to do. It's the human thing. Help someone across the street, shovel your neighbor's driveway, carry groceries for a mom who has her hands full with her kids, cut the grass of someone you know is working three jobs and is too busy to do it. One of my favorites is to randomly pay for people's meals. Whenever I see a police officer in a restaurant, I try to buy their meal. Those guys have a hard job and they are giving to us every single day in their work. We need to be grateful and show appreciation where we can!

I also have a different approach to gift-giving in general. I believe that small random acts of kindness and unexpected gifts are more impressive than things that are expected. I don't give birthday presents or Christmas presents. Instead, the gifts I give are random and because I want to make someone's day.

My city has a football team, the Hamilton Tiger Cats. I have tickets so if I know someone is a fan but wouldn't be able to afford to go otherwise, I give them tickets.

New in the Neighborhood

Hanging out with the Abundance Group and running the Basket Brigade may be the most dramatic ways my life has changed, but the most important is the home life I can offer my kids now. Instead of walking down a street lined with prostitutes, drug dealers, and addicts, my kids live in a neighborhood with doctors, teachers, or lawyers living in every house. Sometimes I'm amazed at how much respect they show me. They know what I do for a living and where I came from, and they totally support me.

My kids can play catch in the street. We leave the front door unlocked. Nobody ever shows up at our door with a baseball bat. The cars are shiny and new, not falling-apart junkers you have to push down the street.

The biggest advantage for my kids is that they get to grow up with two totally on-duty parents. It's a very different atmosphere than I had growing up. My kids are not growing up hungry. They are learning to do their own laundry, but they don't have to go to the laundromat to do it. If the machine breaks down, we fix it. Right away. They don't have to worry about that. Their worries are their grades and their sports. They are getting straight As. They *enjoy* school. They like it! They're self-motivated to do their homework, and they never try to sneak in a sick day. We have to *make* them stay home when they're sick.

We teach our kids things my parents never taught me, like how to stay away from drugs and alcohol. I was buying my father's cigarettes, but my son actually left a friend's house because he was smoking weed. He got up and left! He does not want to be around that stuff. He's seen what drugs have done to some of our renters so he avoids it.

We give 100 percent to whatever our kids are interested in, whether it's drawing or volleyball. I don't think my son needs to take over my business. He should do what he wants to do. I don't want him to have to do it for the money, like I did.

My wife is a true mama bear. I think she gives 1,000 percent. My mom defended me but not in the right way. She wanted to protect me, but her way was to fight. My wife protects our kids, but she doesn't fight. The kids see that, and they don't get in fights either. They've been in arguments but no fights. They've never even seen the inside of a principal's office, a place that was my second home in school.

My son is now bigger than his bullies, but he remembers what it was like to be little. He calls out bullying when he sees it and has a wide variety of friends as a result. I'm very proud of him.

When I go to parent-teacher conferences, all of the talk is positive. I can't believe it. That's not what my mom heard when I was in school. It was always about how much trouble I was in, except the one teacher who recognized me as a young entrepreneur. My kids' conferences are so positive, I joke with the teachers that I'll have to make them say something negative just so we have something to work on!

My kids have mentors all around them. Their neighbors, their teachers, and their parents. They're in an environment that shows them all the possibilities.

Every kid should have mentors to help them on their way. I get mad because I see other kids, just like me, who don't even know they have an opportunity to change things. They don't believe they can succeed. They don't even know it's possible. Until I met my girlfriend who lived up on the mountain, I had no idea other people lived differently. We need to take the less fortunate kids out of their neighborhoods, show them what's out there.

The best mentors I had recognized my unique strengths and passions. They saw the entrepreneur in me. They didn't try to steer me to things I wasn't into. We need to stop teaching everyone the same stuff, and find out what individual kids are good at. Keep them moving in the right direction, and they'll learn to love life. They'll build a better future.

Right now, we only support certain futures. If you're a basketball star, your coaches will teach and encourage you. Same if you're a great student. But what if you're great at sales, or wiring, or plumbing? We need people to teach kids how to excel in these things too. The great thing is, people who are passionate about what they're doing *love* to share it with others so they make excellent mentors.

I know what it's like when you're young. Following your passion doesn't seem to pay the bills. Maybe you will have to go work at McDonald's for a while, even though that's probably not your passion. Okay, fine. Work at McDonald's but do self-development too. Look at what you're passionate about. Find someone who's already successful at that thing and learn from them. You want to be an artist, find an artist who's passionate about the work. You want to be a police officer, go down to the station and check it out. You'll learn so much.

I also know what it's like as a parent. I don't know anything about my children's passions: Marine biology, veterinary medicine, teaching, law enforcement—these are things they are interested in. I don't know anything about those things, but I can help them find the people who do know about these jobs. That's fine. There's no reason your kid should be just like you. I wasn't like my dad, and my kids aren't like me. They're their own individual selves.

Aside from passions, I wish schools taught more of the things that matter in life. Teach the kids how to pay bills and do their taxes. How about insurance? Do they know how to handle money? Do they understand how to handle a household budget? We need people in schools to step up and teach these things.

CHAPTER 10

BOATS AND ROLEXES— GETTING YOUR GOALS

When you're sitting in poverty, surrounded by people who are mean and miserable, there isn't much to focus your attention on the possibilities if you don't do it yourself.

Goal-setting has been the single most powerful tool I've used to get from my upbringing to where I am today. Goals help you avoid the "wish I had" thoughts and turn them into "how can I get" thoughts, which are much more productive.

I help my own kids with this by getting them to create their own vision boards. I tell them to look at the things they want to do that will make them happy, and separate them into these categories:

- Health
- Personal
- Career

My son has a vision board with fancy cars, vacations with the family, playing in the Canadian Football League, and being a teacher.

My daughter has things on her board about being an actress and a marine biologist.

Once the vision board is done, we're not done. I now chat with them about what they have to do to achieve their dreams. I post sticky notes on the walls in their bedroom about what they need to do.

I also encourage them to set small goals. It's not just about large ones. It's not easy to really get excited about a boat when you're 12. So think about something small that you can achieve that you can then celebrate. What is something that you have to do to get to the bigger goal that you can achieve in the next month or three months?

What smaller goal can you achieve first? You have to learn how it feels to accomplish the things you set out to do. That will help you build confidence for the next bigger goal that you'll have.

That's kind of what I did as a kid. When I was 12 years old, my goals were to have a satellite dish to watch every sports game, have a boat, wear a Rolex watch, and to own real estate or be a landlord. But I would shoot for smaller goals and celebrate those wins.

It wasn't exactly a well-rounded vision for my future. There were no health, fitness, or sports goals in my dream. It was all about stuff I wanted.

But I achieved all the goals except the Rolex watch. It's hard to buy such an expensive item to wear on my wrist. It's not that I couldn't buy one right now but I have other uses for that money. Someday I'll get one.

Some of my goals have turned out to be really stupid. Maybe not stupid, but knowing what I know now, they definitely were not in my best interest. My goal for quite some time was to pay off my home and live mortgage free.

For me, and what I am trying to do in the bigger picture of my life, the goal was so opposite of what it should have been. I'm not saying having a mortgage and using the excess money to buy things like Rolex watches is a good plan but taking the money from my home and buying good assets with it is much smarter. It is making money off your money. So that's not my goal anymore. And that is okay. I learned how dumb it was and changed it.

Once you've set your bigger goal you have to break it down into smaller goals. Then you have to look at them weekly.

Let's say you want to own and drive a Ferrari but right now you ride the bus. How are you going to get there? First, maybe, you need to get a second job. Break that goal down, plan on the first step, and then the next step.

The most important thing is to change your attitude.

Change the mindset of "I can't afford" to asking yourself, "How can I buy it? What do I have to do to be able to buy that watch?"

That's how I build out my goals.

Then posting your goals where you see them is important so you can spend time visualizing the achievement of those goals. I could see myself on the boat, wearing the Rolex watch, going on vacation with my family.

Visualizing it is important because it helps you build the belief that it can be your life. That you can achieve this, but you have to get to work on actually getting it on a daily basis and believe that you are going to do it. Believe in it. Want it. And that visualization can become a reality.

And when you get to those goals you've set out, you have to reward yourself. Celebrate it. Make it exciting. It's too easy to achieve something and quickly move onto the next thing, but that isn't feeding your brain to achieve more and more goals as well as you can.

Is it worth achieving if you aren't going to celebrate it?

CHAPTER 11
IT'S TIME TO ACT—WE NEED YOU MORE THAN EVER

There's moral outrage when child abuse is in the media. Everyone is quick to declare their disgust and demand action be taken. But how many people see a child in a home where they aren't loved or there isn't security? Maybe negative behaviors like fighting and stealing are encouraged and obvious. Still, people turn away. Maybe it's because they aren't sure what to do or whether the child really needs help.

I hope what I've shared will show you that the child does need you.

My childhood wasn't unique. In fact, at many points in writing this book I stopped because I thought, "So many people have my story—why tell it?" I nearly quit this book completely during the editing because I am fully expecting to be told that it's a piece-of-shit book and I only wrote it to get pity.

Thankfully, I was reminded that the reason I wrote this

book was for the one kid that might be helped. And the fact that there are a lot of people with my story is exactly why I need to write this book.

It would be nice to know that it was just me and my family that were like this, but one out of three kids in Canada are likely in some sort of abusive or dangerous situation.[4] You might think that there are government agencies or "other people" that will do something to prevent the kind of childhood I had, but they won't. My life wasn't good, but it's not the kind of life that government agencies warrant bad enough to remove the kids from their parents.

A situation has to be really bad for a kid to be removed from their family. From what I have seen, it's usually star athletes or extremely dangerous situations that get attention. I was paying my parents' mortgage, working some family scams, and getting into fights. These are not good things, but they aren't exactly things that will get a kid rescued from their situation.

But these are things that have a lifelong impact on a child. Even today, while I have worked really hard and I've come a long way as far as what I believe I am capable of and what I have done, I still second-guess myself. For example, I am confident with my real estate dealings, but when it comes to something new like writing this book, all the childhood wounds open up and I don't think I'm good enough.

And remember how 30 percent of the population waits

[4] https://www150.statcan.gc.ca/n1/daily-quotidien/170216/dq170216b-eng.htm.

until later to report they were abused? A lot of those people were kids when they were abused. It's not a bad enough situation that the police get called in. These situations are just not going to help a kid ever live up to the potential that they have.

And the worst part is that when you're bullied or your parents don't believe in you as a kid, you carry that with you for life. Those are wounds and scars that impact everything you do. When you're being bullied, especially by your family, you fill your head with negativity. You aren't looking at your parents or the people around you wondering what is wrong with them that they would treat a kid so badly. You're looking in the mirror and thinking, "Everything is wrong with me and nobody likes me." The bad treatment makes you feel like you don't deserve anything good.

You feel like you deserve that treatment!

And when you grow up feeling like you deserve to be treated like crap, it's really hard to become a confident, contributing adult.

If that kid is you right now, I believe in you. You're reading this so you already know there is a better life available to you. Life is hard, but you are worthy. And it's not your fault that you've been treated badly. You're going to doubt yourself and wonder if you deserve anything good that might happen. Please know that you deserve it. You will have to work hard and get it. But it's there. I promise. Nobody will give it to you. You have to go and get it. You have to get away from your old life and relationships because they will always try to pull you down.

Even when you've left, they will always try to pull you down.

Remember that as you start to dream bigger. As I said, I almost gave up on this book so many times because I kept hearing those old voices.

After reading this, I hope you realize how important you are and how much we need you.

We need you to believe in yourself. Your kids need you to believe in yourself and believe in a better life for you and everyone around you. Find something you love and are passionate about and chase it. And try to find friends who want great things for you and share those passions with them. Keep your distance from those who will keep you down, criticize you for trying, or try to take every dollar you make.

Have dreams and reach for them.

We need you to know that you can do anything regardless of your background.

It's not just me who has overcome a tough upbringing to find happiness and success doing something I love. Oprah Winfrey spoke openly about the violent physical and emotional abuse she suffered as a child.[5] Howard Schulz, founder of Starbucks, grew up in a housing complex for the poor.[6] Now he uses what he built to do what-

---

[5] https://www.dailymail.co.uk/tvshowbiz/article-2239102/Oprah-Winfrey-opens-traumatic-childhood-David-Letterman-lecture-series.html.

[6] https://www.businessinsider.com/billionaires-who-came-from-nothing-2013-12#starbucks-founder-howard-schultz-grew-up-in-a-housing-complex-for-the-poor-5.

ever he can to support veterans and people of all races and provide jobs for underprivileged youth.[7]

Oprah and Howard Schulz are billionaires today.

Warrick Dunn, 12-year veteran of the NFL who played for the Buccaneers and Falcons, was raised by a single mother. He was one of six kids, and she always dreamed of owning a home for her family. She was a police officer, and she was killed off-duty when he was only 18 years old. He became the head of the house at 18 and raised his siblings. He said they only got by because the community supported them, and that made him realize how important it was to support his community. When he started in the NFL, he began a program that gives away houses to single parents. To date, he's given away 159 houses to single parents who need a home.[8]

You don't have to be famous to call your life a success. I just want you to see that each of these people found their passion and fought hard to get it. They didn't look around expecting handouts. People may have helped them along the way, but they worked for what they have, and they did not let their origins decide where they can go and what they can do.

It's a guarantee they worked hard every day. I don't know them, but I know what it takes. And I am sure they had to ignore a lot of people who tried to hold them back and keep them from growing.

---

[7] https://www.usnews.com/news/us/articles/2018-06-04/starbucks-chairman-howard-schultz-stepping-down.

[8] https://www.si.com/nfl/2018/01/19/nfl-warrick-dunn-homes-holidays-habitiat-humanity-deshaun-watson.

We need you to ignore the naysayers. We need your inner voice to be louder. The belief you have in yourself to be louder than anything anyone else can say.

We need you to realize that anybody who says horrible things to you is talking about themselves.

And finally…

We need you to be a part of our great societal family because you're important and it wouldn't be the same without you.

Acknowledgments

Publishing a book is a team effort. No author could ever do it alone.

I'd like to thank my wife, Crystal. She believed in me from the day we met – even when I purchased a house without her seeing it or knowing about it until after I did the deal. She trusted me and saw me for who I am. She believed I could do whatever I put my mind to. Even to this day she still has my back 100%.

I'd like to thank Erwin Szeto for telling me to write the book in the first place. Erwin is the kind of guy that pushes you to find new ways to succeed and then holds you accountable to do it. Everyone needs an Erwin in their life and I'm lucky to call him a friend.

Finally, I'd like to thank Book Launchers, who helped get this book from an idea to a physical book I can hold in my hands. They were dedicated to getting my book finished to the highest standard.

CPSIA information can be obtained
at www.ICGtesting.com
Printed in the USA
BVHW090115030620
580577BV00004B/15